Damned if You Do

Damned if You Do

Whether you are partnered or solo, there are joys and pleasures, sacrifices and aggravations *either way*. The strongest partnership is the one you build with yourself.

Dr. Scotia Stone

ISBN 978-1-257-91647-4

This book is dedicated to my grandmother,
Audrea Burns, one of the great loves of my life

Contents

Welcome

Let me begin by telling you about myself. Not because I am so fascinating (well, I think I am!) but because my perspective, my stories, form the backbone of this book. Professionally, I have over 20 years experience in life coaching, human resources, teaching psychology and management, and communication skills consulting. In my late 20s, I earned a doctorate in adult development and developed a specialty in attitudinal change, particularly in counseling adults through life transitions. My coaching work addresses questions such as "How do we create the right relationships in our life? How do we move on from life's inevitable losses? What choices help us grow into the best person we can be?" These questions aren't easy to answer. Over the years, I have counseled and coached hundreds of men and women on such self-development issues.

As far as my personal life, ten years ago, I left my husband and went through a divorce. Since then, I've been raising a son as a single parent, and while I've had a few serious relationships since my divorce, I have yet to remarry. I've been on at least 200 fruitless dates, and also spent way too much time in relationships that weren't working. I thought I would remarry and have another child when I was in my 30s. That was what I wanted, yet neither of these things happened. Five years ago, I was diagnosed with thyroid cancer, and went through surgery and radiation. This experience opened my eyes to how short life can really be. We all understand this intellectually, but it's very different to get it *emotionally*. Having this experience was a blessing. Unlike so many people who've had cancer, I had time to use my illness as a motivator to make changes in my life.

The idea for this book came out of my longing to share my stories, my "tales from the front", so that other women might benefit from my travails. While I coach both men and women, I particularly wanted to offer women's stories and insights into how to craft better relationships and better lives. When I listen to the women I counsel, I'm always struck by how far along a continuum of self development they all are. I think if only Lisa, whose husband just left her, could hear Susan's story she'd see how divorce can be a rebirth, that no matter how painful it is, it *can* be a bridge to a better life. I've thought if Helen could hear Jenny's story - Jenny who got married for the first time at age 52 - she'd see that while online dating is frustrating, it can lead to the love of your life.

When I left my husband, I received an outpouring of emotional help from a friend who'd been divorced for several years. She was much farther along the continuum than I was. While I took up smoking again, booked myself solid on every weekend I didn't have my son, and basically fought off panic attacks every day, she not only listened to all my anxiety and fear, she also gave me practical ideas for how to make the transition to single life easier. I'll never forget her simple advice to paint my bedroom a new color and then go to TJ Maxx and buy myself new towels, sheets, curtains and a new bedspread. Make a visual transition into my new life. It's a piece of advice I've shared many times since.

There's a saying "People change when the pain of staying the same gets too great." I love this because it points out how we often go kicking and screaming into change. If it was so easy to just read a self-help book and change your life, we'd all have done it. Like many women in the caring professions, I chose this work because I wanted to help people make positive changes, but I also wanted to heal my own demons. Despite my education and experience, I have the same insecurities, fears and disappointments in relationships that other women have. Like some of you I grew up with abuse, alcoholism, and other family dynamics that were hard to overcome. Just because I understood psychological growth, and could counsel other women on it, did not mean I could always make those changes myself. It's taken me many years, and a lot of heartache to get to where I am now. Yet, at this vantage point, I see that while I've paid a cost, I've earned a lot of peace and pride too.

That is the perspective I want to share with you, not from some lofty authoritative position, but from a place of commonality. I've observed in my professional and personal life how therapeutic sharing stories with other women can be. It's comforting to hear that we are not alone; other women have been through this too. It helps us to learn what worked for them and what they learned along the way. They survived, and often thrived. So can you. Whether it's with problems at work, with friends, or romantic relationships, other women's stories help soothe and inspire. They make the journey a little less perilous.

That is the spirit of this book.

Damned if You Do

There is this ongoing conversation that I have with a myriad of friends and family members. We get talking about our marriages or our dating life or lack thereof. We compare notes on other friend's situations, or things we heard in the news. Which celebrities hooked up or broke up this week. Then as the conversation winds down, that phrase always comes out with a heavy sigh. Ah. "You're damned if you do." Like either way, it's always something.

It seems that no matter which situation you are in- single or partnered- there are certain pleasures and joys, pressures and aggravations. I've been in both situations and for me the verdict is still out. Partnering is the goal, what everyone seems to want. Companionship and sexual expression, a soul mate, a sounding board. Someone to help raise kids, share your trials and tribulations, grow old with. Just be WITH. Coupled. Not alone. Who wouldn't want that to help face the harsher realities of modern life? Dating is an anxiety-producing chore; being alone can be lonely. Society continually informs us that couples have it easier. Financially if nothing else. The couple-craze also enforces that your value as a woman depends on your ability to attract a man. If you're so great, but still alone, how come no one wants you? Commitment, especially marriage, sounds like the Holy Grail, the magic key to a better life.

Yet when you are with someone there are the constant challenges of maintaining your couplehood. You and your partner have competing agendas, needs, styles, etc. There are the stressors of managing property and children, work demands, in-law hassles, a sudden illness. There's the risk he'll do things like leave you for your neighbor, or develop an addiction to online porn. I know of many unhappy marriages. I was in one. Compromise isn't always possible, and the risks are high. So many people stay in bad relationships out of fear of losing their money, social standing, connection to children and family. But bad relationships can cost you not only money and time, but your health and sanity as well. We all know chronic stress can bring on illness and disease. So no less than your life is at stake here, really.

When I got married, I was in my 20s and all my friends were still single. When I'd hear their stories, I envied single girl life. God, it sounded like fun. Meeting tons of men at parties, art openings, clubs, the gym. Going out every night of the week if they wanted to. Then when they'd have yet another demoralizing breakup story, as they always did, I'd become what Bridget Jones called the "smug marrieds." Those married couples who say things like "Oh, you poor thing, dating does just suck, doesn't it!" I'd silently thank the universe that it wasn't me. Thank god I don't have to go through that dating hell!

This duality has always hit me the worst on Friday nights. Unhappily married, I dreaded coming home after a long work week to a dull night of a pizza and a DVD. I wished I could have been in the city, out on the town with my friends. Then these last ten years, often coming home alone on a Friday evening, I wish I had someone to cuddle with, shed the cares of the week with…order a pizza and watch a DVD!

When I'm single, I miss affection and companionship. I get tired of having to make social plans rather than knowing I have my partner to hang out with. I hate being asked, like so many single women are- "Why are you still single?"

Yet it's not all bad. I am far more productive when I'm single. My assistant said this to me years ago after yet another breakup and it struck a chord. "I know you like having a boyfriend, but you are so much happier when you don't have one," she said, shaking her head.

I remind myself of this. When I'm totally single, I eat better, I sleep better, I exercise more. I'm an analytical person-I obsess a lot less. And I think of the years I was married, and one post-divorce boyfriend I lived with for several months. And both times I ended up feeling trapped. Not every day, but enough.

Of course, however you fall in this equation, each person is only one person away from being alone. You can find what you seek- true love, true connection - but never know what will happen after that. He could get hit by a car, fall in love with someone else, you may fall out of love, one of you could get a debilitating illness. Every day is a new day. Every day you wake up and get to make choices about how to conduct your life. So, you are never *really* stuck, or a victim of fate.

So, you've heard it before. Life, love, is all a crap shoot and there are no guarantees. The relationship you have with yourself is the most important one you'll ever have. Because it's the only one you have your whole life. Therefore, as Shakespeare says, before all, to thine own self be true.

While this book is for every woman struggling with the tensions between being partnered and being solo, I wrote this book with a special focus on women who like me, have been both. There is a certain painful loss when a marriage ends, yet a certain kind of optimism emerges too. It's happened for you before, it'll happen again, if you want it to. And when you come to the dating table, you bring all your hard won experiences and insights. I think we can all learn something from this unique vantage point.

In this book, I stress certain points continuously, all centered around having persistence, drive and determination for finding the relationship you want. I also try to provide humor and insight on how to create the *life* you want, with optimism, faith and positive expectations. Last, and I'll say this again and again, ultimately the most important relationship is the one you build with yourself.

And in that, you're never damned if you do.

Holding in High Esteem

Suddenly I see, this is what I want to be...

-K.T. Tunstall

Before you roll your eyes, let me say that this chapter just has to be in here. It is the underpinning of everything that goes afoul in our lives. All women struggle with low self esteem, in some way, shape or form. It often seems that any woman growing up in this culture has issues with something - love hunger, body image, shopping addiction, etc. etc. American culture is not particularly affirming to women - just read *Glamour, Shape, People, Vogue*, the list goes on. I love chilling with a fresh magazine as much as the next girl, but every article is about what we are not doing wrong or what we could do better. Self improvement is great but often by the time you hit the back cover, you're convinced that you're overweight, you smell bad, you need a new wardrobe, and people don't actually like you after all. Magazines sell advertising. Insecure women buy a lot more products.

Not only is our culture more affirming to men, many of us grew up in homes where men made all the decisions, or sons were treated better. I know several women in their 50s and 60s whose brothers got to go to college, but they were told an education would be wasted on them because they'd only get married and not use it. Women still make less money than men, 76 cents on the dollar. Trust me, I've worked in Human Resources. Even if we survived middle school, we still came away with the message that our worth is measured by how big our butt isn't. We have to continually worry about being victims of rape or abuse in ways men do not. It's tough out there. And saying so is not a great feminist manifesto. It's true. So even if we personally feel great- solid, strong-there are forces in our culture that will try to keep us feeling insecure, and like we are not doing well without a man around.

Another contributing factor to our low self esteem is that most women have a hard time handling conflict. Over the years, I have sent many women to the Skillpath "Conflict Management for Women" seminar. The place is always packed. And no doubt, every woman there learns something. Growing up, we are rarely taught how to assert ourselves, or how to negotiate. We are taught to fear being called selfish, or a bitch. We're not told you can disagree with someone and still be liked, in fact often liked and respected far more.

This causes us to constantly second guess ourselves in our relationships- Are we being a bitch? Are we too powerful? Do we intimidate men? I've known many beautiful and smart female doctors, lawyers, business owners who struggle with this one. If they were men, the women would be all over them. Their education and career would make them a real catch. I've often joked about myself this way. If I were a tall and attractive divorced **man** with a doctorate, who went to good schools, made good money, owned a nice home, had a great son, they'd be beating a path to my door. But those same qualities in a woman can seem like a liability.

I've had many people say to me personally "Boy, I'm sure you're intimidating to a man." Why? Because I have a lot of education? Because I'm tall? Because I'm outspoken? Supposedly, men don't want women who make more money than them, or have more education, or more societal respect. We all know many successful, accomplished men who don't care what a woman does. She could be a prostitute, live on the dole, whatever. So long as it's not more prestigious than them. Why wouldn't a successful man want his equal? If he's smart and savvy with his resources, wouldn't he want someone who brings something to the table too?

I know there *are* many men who want their equal, and now that women have more educational and career opportunities, they can find her. But there is still the issue of whose career dominates the partnership, when it comes time for a job relocation, or for staying home to raise kids. Many women still feel societal pressure to put husbands and kids first.

Women prioritize relationships. We want them. Despite all the books that tell us how fabulous we are alone, or all the people who tell you you'll meet a guy when you're not looking and "least expect it", we do love *loving*, and we feel more alive when we are sharing our lives with someone. It doesn't mean we can't live without it, just that we will make certain sacrifices for it. I have. I assume you have. Like overlooking that he has huge debt. Or has three ex-wives. Or that he never listens when we are talking. Or calls when he says he will. Every woman likes having someone to hold her and kiss her, likes having a

Saturday night date. And someone to call if her car breaks down, other than AAA.

We not only want a man, we feel judged when we don't have one. As a single woman, you meet so many people who say things like "You're so funny! You're so attractive! Boy, you're great!" then the old "I can't believe you haven't found a man!" My personal favorite is "How come you're not married?", which is often asked in a suspicious tone, like you're hiding some fatal flaw. I like to point out that I did snare a man, I just returned him to the universe in my divorce. The whole message is offensive because it is so pitying. "Gee, what is wrong with you? I feel so bad for you." I've actually had people say to me "Don't worry. You'll find someone." And they follow up with "I wish I knew a guy to set you up with!" Like you're going to commit suicide if they don't personally find you a date for Friday night.

Even some men I know say things like that. "I wish I knew someone to set you up with but all the single guys I know are assholes." Great.

The worst offenders are the women who were single for a long time and are now married. They say things that make you feel like you're on an episode of *Survivor*. "Boy, I'm glad I made immunity and didn't have to eat the worm larvae. Too bad you did." Married women love your dating stories, yet when you're done they say something like "Oh, being single is *so* awful!" I had lunch with a college friend once who said, verbatim, "I was so afraid I'd never be married. No one wanted me. I'm so glad Doug saved me from that." And the woman is a partner in a law firm, accomplished in her own right.

Now I know people mean well. I know that is where most of these comments come from. Women like everyone to be settled. Everyone paired, everybody happy. And I like when people take me under their wing to the extent that they set me up with someone. That is the best way to meet people. You get to do a little vetting. So, if I have to take a little condescension to meet the guy of my dreams, so be it. I've certainly accepted far worse from guys I was actually dating. Yet it perpetuates the notion that your value is as a half of a couple, not just as you, a member of society.

Another problem with this viewpoint is it only focuses on arrival, the ring, not on the process of building a good relationship. Getting married is not the right goal. Finding the right life partner is.

Because we are judged by society on whether we are partnered or not, breakups can be particularly brutal to your sense of self worth. If society judges on us whether a man wants us, and we judge our lovability by the success of our relationships, there is a huge loss in no longer being half of a couple. Even if you were the one who did the breaking. There is your private grief- you can't believe it's over. You tried so hard to make it work. Will it take forever to meet someone else? This is the death of all your hopes! And there is the public mourning. You used to show up places with a man in tow. Now you're stag. Everyone keeps asking "Where's so and so?" You have to relive the end all over again, mumbling some lame retort like "Oh, we were growing in different directions….." As if anyone believes that one. That loss of a husband or boyfriend can set your self esteem back for months, even years.

There are so many ways women blame themselves when they are broken up with, thinking "if I were smarter, prettier, nicer…" he wouldn't have left me. You know intellectually that's not it. I want to print and sell bumper stickers that say "It's not you. It's him." How about *he's* not worthy of *you*?

Put differently, we can see this self-blame as a desire for control. If it's us, something in us that caused him to leave, we think we could have fixed it. Which is, of course, rarely true. In college, I worked for a woman who found out after two kids and 20 years of marriage that her husband was gay. This happens with some frequency, sad to say. Could this woman have done something differently so her husband would become straight? Of course not! So why do we think we can change other things about people, like their drinking too much, or their poor spending habits or their cheating heart? We don't have that kind of power.

I once overheard two women having lunch in the booth behind me at my favorite restaurant. One was describing her recent breakup, and all the problems her ex-boyfriend had. She said she tried so hard to help him, but he just resented her. The other woman was nodding sympathetically, then she said "Well, it sounds like he just needs to be with someone more screwed up than you." The break-up woman sighed "Yeah, I guess so." But you could tell she was really sad about it, rather than seeing him as sad that he needed to be with a screwed up person to feel good about himself.

Somewhere within us we must think we don't deserve any more. Our self esteem is low enough to settle for this sub-par creature, and for sub-par treatment. One of the most profound comments anyone ever made to me was ten years ago, just after my divorce. I was at my friend Carol's house, as always prattling on and on about David, this difficult, somewhat cruel labor lawyer I was dating. After one of my particularly whiny and winded sentences, Carol looked at me and said "You keep telling me you want to be loved, but you must not, because you stay with someone who is so clearly incapable of loving." Wow. It was *me*. Not him.

So, me…. I could fix me. And you can fix you. In fact, the energy and effort you expend on a bad relationship is far better spent on yourself. That is how we can counteract this over-focus on him. Own what is yours. For me, that meant recognizing my codependence. That I chose men who were remote and incapable of being loving and present with me. That I chose guys like this because I was trying to avoid intimacy too. It's the same as losing weight or putting more energy into your appearance. All the "find a man when you're 80" books tell you that you have to remove barriers to a man being attracted to you. Fair enough. You have to be brutally honest with yourself about those physical barriers, but the *emotional* ones too. What has kept you in a bad relationship, what dependency, fear of abandonment, or low sense of self worth? Figure that out. Because then you can have control, the healthy kind. The control over your own mind, the ability to change what isn't working and stop hurting yourself by refusing to suffer in a bad relationship. Put all that energy you put into him into yourself and your life will change.

To do this, you have to figure out where the desire for a man like this comes from, why you want him. Simply put, many of us recreate childhood dramas in our romantic life. We choose an alcoholic just like Dad. Or a cold and remote man whose approval we seek, just like we did with Mom. We think subconsciously we can win this time. And we will be just as hurt and frustrated when we don't.

In this process, we must have compassion for ourselves. When we feel weak, we shouldn't compound it by also feeling shame. You already feel bad enough, and you shouldn't. Because it's all about progress, not perfection. You are doing the best you can. And one way out of this mental trap? Commend your progress. You have come a long way. You have, no doubt, made improvements in your life. As Maya Angelou says, "When you know better, you do better." When you learn to like and respect yourself, you value yourself, and you will not put up with the same crap anymore. Remember, this is a lifelong process. You are never done. Like when you lose 20 pounds- are you done then? No, you have to maintain it. You can't just go back to not exercising and eating everything in sight. Relationship successes are the same way. They require maintenance. Vigilance.

In struggling to end my last relationship, and to truly let him go, I used to feel crazy and mad with grief. I couldn't understand why. Ian was a jerk- cold, depressed, self absorbed, horrible with money, skittish on commitment. Why wasn't I happy it was over? I had tried to end it myself for months. It was love addiction, trying to get this emotionally unavailable man to love me, when he was incapable. But I realized one day- I have made progress. Five years before, when I'd been in a similar relationship with a similar man, Nick, I wouldn't let go. I kept trying to make it work, and kept getting back together with him. Now I wasn't holding on. Progress!

The point here is - ok, there are several. First off, no man will save you. We are all old enough now to get that. You may want him and love him, and bless him if he is good to you, and it is all great-the long talks, the weekend trips, the sex -but you are still alone. It is your life, and up to only you to make it what you want and need it to be. Second, you have got to hold out for what you want. Like a job, or a great suit, the good ones are not as prevalent as the simply ok ones. I grew up on the ocean, so let me use a fishing metaphor. If you want to land a swordfish, you can't keep filling your boat up with perch. You have to believe in yourself, like yourself, enough to know that good things can and will come to you. You have to have space in your life for them to come into. Likewise, when you take a chance on a man and he turns out not to have your best interests at heart, or is incapable of giving you what you need, throw him back in the sea. Every extra day you are with the wrong man keeps you from meeting the right one.

I read this quote once, I forgot where- "A bad man is a gift that teaches you, through torment, to love yourself." You learn to value yourself and fight for yourself in the act of letting go of him. In listening to that intuitive voice that says "I deserve better than this."

Yes, it is hard. But it is all up to you. That said, let's look a little deeper at you.

Locking on

I am a voracious reader. I love learning new things. Particularly psychological stuff – I'm not that interested in quantum physics or how to assess the gross domestic product. Understanding why and how things occur *emotionally*, the life inside the mind, is far more interesting to me. Why do people do what they do? I want to know. Having information gives me a sense of control and peace. Even better, if I can understand why *I* think the way I do, I can learn a new way to look at things and make positive changes in my life.

Over twenty years ago, I was in an abusive relationship with a college boyfriend. He yelled at me constantly, belittled me, cheated on me, even kicked me once. I was madly in love, and could not shake his hold on me, no matter how cruel he became. During this time, my grandmother sent me a copy of Robin Norwood's book *Women Who Love Too Much*. I skimmed through it and thought this is not me. And I put it aside. Over ten years later, after I'd left my husband and gotten involved with an emotionally abusive man yet again, I picked it back up and this time it all made sense.

Now there are many great books on love and sex addiction, as well as on obsessive love. My favorite is Susan Peabody's *Addiction to Love*. I won't repeat all of what these books say but let me offer this-love addiction is what so many of us struggle with having been raised in a home where our emotional needs weren't met. Whether it was due to divorce, illness, death, addiction to drugs or alcohol, neglect or just plain emotional unavailability of her caregiver, a girl with love addiction didn't learn to believe in herself or that she is worthy of love. So as an adult she chooses and stays with men who aren't good for her. Couple that with the fact that we often choose partners like our unavailable parent so that we can "win" this time around. Get them to love us like they weren't able to when we were kids. What greater thrill for someone struggling with self worth than to get the unloving to love you?

So many times when I was in my unhealthy relationships, I would talk to friends who seemed to have boyfriends and husbands who were emotionally healthy, who were giving and present. Once I got over my surprise – There is a man like that out there?– I'd feel envy. How did she get so lucky? It took me about 25 years to realize **I** was the one staying in unsatisfying relationships, locked on to an unhealthy guy. I was doing it to myself.

We all wonder why women stay with the men they do. You hear their tales of woe and think yuck, why on earth does she put up with that? The worst case scenario is domestic violence– we hear stories on the news and wonder what was wrong with her that she didn't leave? Or we hear milder tales – women who are staying with men who cheat on them or women who are constantly belittled and controlled by their partners.

There are lots of reasons why we put up with it. It all stems from the same low self-worth, just varying degrees of it. Low self worth, and also FEAR. Fear of being alone. It feels like he is the last man who will ever love us. If he leaves, we'll have nothing. Fear of abandonment, because we were abandoned, emotionally or physically, as children. Fear of loss is powerful. Particularly for those of us who associate longing with love, who are not used to our emotional needs being met by anyone. It is incredibly hard to let go, even when the relationship is painful and clearly not working. It feels like another confirmation that we are not lovable. You stay with him, miserable in the relationship yet unable to leave. That pull, that fear of abandonment, can be excruciating. It's like an alcoholic trying not to drink. Or a gambler trying not to gamble. You know you shouldn't do it but you can't help yourself.

What's also operating is we think we've invested too much time and energy to bail out now. It is so hard to let go of the thing that we have worked for, even if what we are doing isn't working. It is also hard to ignore his needs and moods. It's in our nature to want to help. To soothe. To solve. We can't understand why we aren't able to love this man into wholeness. We love him so much, why can't that heal him?

This inability to let go keeps us from finding the person and situation that is right for us. So often women ask the wrong question – why do I keep meeting bad men? Well, there are bad men out there. The answer is you will always meet them. They are there. Yet it is *what you do about it* that makes a difference. If you choose to get involved and to stay, you accept the bad relationship with the bad man. And that is in your control. You are not a victim of fate.

It's easy to feel that you are. It's easy to feel doomed, like this stuff is just so much of your emotional programming that you are never going to get better and you will always have to deal with heartache. It's easy to feel like a victim. This is incredibly unfair that this happened to me and it's all everyone else's fault. Yes, it is unfair. Yet as we all know, fairness was not a guarantee we were given when we popped onto this earth.

Now back to love addiction. Women like me, and maybe you, didn't grow up with the sense that we were loved simply for who we were. We were ignored, or abused, or shamed. Thus, even now, we feel unlovable deep down. We get drawn to people whose fear of intimacy is just as great as our own. We stay with men who allow us to avoid intimacy because for whatever reason- an addiction, being married to someone else, living in another country or in prison, being emotionally shut down- they aren't really available either. A real and present partner, who wants to fully be there for us, can make us uncomfortable. And chances are high we won't find him attractive anyway. He's too present, too *nice*.

One way we escape from our negative emotions is through relationship addiction, through overfocusing on our love life. We overfocus on other people in a myriad of ways- by controlling what our husband wears, by telling our kids what to say to their friends, by insisting our neighbor use our landscaper, on and on. From the mild to the extreme. But with romantic relationships, we harbor the secret belief that having a romantic partner can make all our other problems go away. So we focus even more on these relationships.

A great quote from *Addiction to Love* sums this up:

> *The core satisfaction with love addiction is not so much the particular pleasure experienced with a specific man, but the escape provided from daily anxiety or frustration. Love addicts are most frequently women for whom the world seems bleak, empty and fraught with perils...love addictions represent poorly understood attempts by women to solve problems of self worth, completion and personal validation. Relief from these deep feelings of insecurity is found in the thoughts, feelings and fantasies these women have about men* (Peabody, 2006, p. 25).

There is another insidious element at work here too- we want to win. We see relationships as a challenge. There is the challenge I already mentioned, about getting the love of an unavailable person, the feeling that you'll conquer those inner demons because you are going to win this time. That's the heart of it. But it's also women's general emotional competitiveness with the world, the same zeitgeist that compels us to be the greatest friend, the best wife, the most awesomest baker of cookies at our kid's school. Once committed, we won't back down from the battle.

Even if it feels bad, we are used to it. Having suffered lack of healthy love our whole lives, suffering feels normal. You've heard the analogy about cooking a frog. If you put it in the pot and you turn on the burner, the water heats over time, the frog gets comfortable and doesn't notice. If we threw the frog in when it was already boiling, it would have jumped out. We have gotten comfortable with the slowly boiling water, even though it's going to kill us.

So how do you get out of the pot? Jump.

Your job is to take care of you. Plain and simple. I remember reading a line in *Women Who Love Too Much* that touched on this so well. "When you take all that energy that you were focusing on him and give it to yourself, life will change." Change your focus to yourself, learn to give all that wonderful care and support to *you* first. And things will improve. Slowly. But they will.

I think of several women I have known, who didn't seem to get the good relationships they deserved:

Erica, who accepts her boyfriend keeping another full time girlfriend because she knows eventually he'll commit to her because she had a baby with him.

Beth, whose husband hasn't worked in five years and sits around smoking pot every day.

Dana, who's lived with her boyfriend for 7 years even though he won't agree to marry her and she wants to get married and have children before it's too late.

Lisa, who stays in a relationship with a married man even when he treats her poorly and says he will never leave his wife.

All of these women are smart, funny and beautiful. They all deserve more. But they all have to be willing to demand more. And that requires a change in themselves.

Over the years, I kept looking at myself, and many women I've coached, wondering if we were doomed to be unlucky in love. If we were always going to be our own worst enemy. I longed for us all to become the type of woman I've seen, albeit rarely, who values herself far too much to stick around. Who truly lets go of things that no longer suit her. Who doesn't worry that nothing else will come along, but believes in herself enough to know it will.

One day I realized I *could become* that kind of woman. It was my choice.

The first self-defeating thing I wanted to change about myself centered around always being busy. If I went into a weekend without my son and without plans, it made me anxious. I would try to find people to socialize with. I always appreciated having a strong network of friends, but I threw too much time into my social life and not enough into the other things that were important- my writing, volunteering, exercising, even keeping a clean house! It's not that I didn't like being alone, I did, but not for long periods of time. I also used to crave the distractions of my romances. Life was pretty dull without some type of intrigue. Without at least something in the pipeline- a date, speculation about a new guy or a resurfacing ex- I was bored.

These same distractions kept me from finishing this book. Kept me from cleaning out my basement. From finding a new auto insurance carrier. All this stuff is very dull. And very responsible. But it is part of my life. Attending to these things is a way of caring for myself.

When I was finally willing to sit still with that uncomfortable feeling, after years of avoiding it, I found it wasn't so bad. By confronting it, over time I began to feel a tremendous peace. Peace, and pride. That I had struggled and prayed, and ultimately found a way to live with that anxiety. That I was able to feel the pain of it yet also appreciate the gift of self awareness that it brought me.

So how do you deal with the things that make you uncomfortable, cause you emotional pain? All you can do is learn about them. Ask questions. Why am I feeling anxious? Why does spending a weekend alone bother me? Why do I feel so angry when he doesn't do what I've asked? Whatever your questions are, don't run from the pain, anxiety and anger they bring up. Open yourself to feeling it and then sit still with it. It won't kill you. Invite it in so you can heal it, then use that newfound strength to make better choices next time.

I share this with you because I want you to know how hard it is. I would far rather eat worm larvae than sit and struggle with these emotions. My grandmother always said you can't put an old head on young shoulders. She'd say this when I was complaining about yet another frustrating romance. She longed to save me from the pain she went through in her two marriages. She couldn't. I can't spare you. It can be a constant journey to overcome pain and frustration in our lives. But there is great peace in knowing you aren't alone. Twelve step programs work for that reason. To be heard and accepted by people who struggle with the same thing you do takes the shame out of it and allows you to move forward. Reading inspirational stories about other women allows you to see how it all came together for them and how it can and will happen for you. For me, studying Buddhism and ways to develop patience and compassion has helped a lot too. Patience was never my strong suit, but I am getting better, and I am first and foremost giving the gift of patience and compassion to myself.

I also want you to be prepared for what it is like to change, to become your better self. It has its moments of joy. That peaceful feeling of "I did this. I worked hard and it came to fruition." Self-acceptance feels great. But it has a price too. I remember a story I heard in a college philosophy class, Plato's *Parable of the Cave*. Essentially, a group of people have lived chained in a cave all of their lives. They watch shadows projected on the wall by things passing in front of the cave entrance, and think these shadows are reality, this is all there is. One day, one person sees that there is light outside the cave, a whole world out there. He tells the others, but they don't believe him. He then faces a difficult choice. To leave the cave for something better means he loses his companions, what is secure. To go out to the light means he heads toward risk and alienation, but also toward self development, enlightenment, knowledge of himself and the world around him. The Parable reminds us that this knowledge has a cost.

When you change, everyone around you has to change. And they usually don't like it. You used to laugh at their dirty jokes. Or not talk back when they criticized you. Or not speak up when they slighted you. Now you don't feel able to overlook certain behaviors or comments. You no longer enjoy spending time with certain people. A feeling creeps over you, of being a stranger in a strange land. A feeling of that is the woman I used to be, but *she doesn't live here any more*, metaphorically speaking! That is the price of change.

Let me give you an example. One of my coaching clients, Marie, is a woman who has undergone a lot of emotional changes in the past year. She's worked hard to improve certain things about herself, through therapy, reading, traveling, time alone. She has always had a lot of friends, and it's been important for her to have several women to be close to. But lately, something has changed with several of her closest friendships. When Marie was around Gail, she always used to have fun- Gail liked to go out to bars, meet people, analyze male behavior over margaritas. Now it seems like *all* Gail wants to talk about is men. Nothing else. Marie sits there now thinking don't we have any other interests? Then there is her friend Susan, who is so strong and always gives great advice. Whatever dilemma Marie would mention, Susan would cut to the chase and tell her how to handle it. Only now Susan's comments seem controlling, and it feels like she isn't listening to her, just judging her and telling her what she is doing wrong. Marie has known her friend Ellie since they were kids, and she always enjoys hanging out with her. But often a month or two goes by and Ellie hasn't called her. Marie thinks about it and realizes that in the last five years, Ellie has never been the one to call and suggest they get together. She always did that. And now she doesn't feel like doing all the work anymore.

None of Marie's friends have changed. Marie has. She's gotten clearer about who and what she wants in her life. What wasn't illuminated before, now is. And what was once acceptable behavior from others, now isn't.

This is the price of change. In clearing your emotional closet, you must let go of that which no longer suits you, to make way for something that is a better fit. It is hard. Giving up the known for the unknown. Yet it is, in the end, always the best bargain you'll ever get.

Welcome to the light.

Why?

Tell me whyyyyahhyyyy...why can't you see this boat is sinking...this boat is sinking....

-Annie Lennox

Life would be easy, wouldn't it, if we didn't have to deal with other people? With their needs and wants, their sensitivities and weaknesses, their complaints and our obligations to fix them. Yes. It would. We are busy enough with work, errands, kids, running a home. Top that off with trying to find a great eye cream, enroll in a pottery class, read let alone write a novel, spend at least some time this month with a girlfriend or two.... We have so much to do for others and never enough time to give to ourselves. We don't need the aggravation of trying to figure out why people do what they do, why other people are so annoying and maddening, and take so much of our mental and physical energy...energy that if we got it back it would allow us to get far more done!

As noted philosopher Jean-Paul Sartre said: hell *is* other people. It isn't a fiery pit with goblins dancing around pulling out your entrails. It's right here. The people who frustrate you.

No where else do we see that as strongly as with the opposite sex. Men. While there are many great men out there, it is the difficult ones who cause us to ask all those frustrated "why?" questions. Why do men do what they do? Or don't do? Why do they say they are going to call and then don't? Why do they date one woman for years, dump her then marry the next woman they meet? Why do they get angry and defensive when you want to talk about your relationship? Why do they chase the pants off you and when you finally give in you never hear from them again? Why?

Because they can.

Like Bill Clinton with Monica Lewinsky, or Bernie Madoff with those stolen billions. Why do they do it? Because they can.

Society tells women that as the keepers of the hearth and home, it is our responsibility to fix a relationship when it isn't working. Sure, men have responsibilities too, but our pressure is far greater. Thus we spend a lot of energy trying to figure out why men do certain things. Yet it's often a futile pursuit because there are certain behaviors and issues though that no matter how loving, wonderful and smart *you* may be, you will never fix in *him*. Really, it is silly for us to think we can, and a little controlling to boot. As if we have the power to change another person. We can't control other people, only our reaction to them.

So in this chapter we'll explore the reasons why our relationships with some men don't work, and why they shouldn't. Because often these issues are too much to bear and you should move on. Sometimes you may choose to stay. Always, it's your choice.

The first reason *why* is that some men should just come with warning labels saying "WARNING! Please read before investing emotional energy!" Because some men are just assholes and everything they do is tainted by their malice. Woman after woman will hear from friends or co-workers that a guy is a jerk, yet they'll still get involved with him. They think that he'll be different with them. As if he has changed. Why would he? What he is doing is working because great woman after great woman goes out with him.

Some other men do things just to spite the woman in their lives. They're passive aggressive, or just aggressive. I'll never forget a dinner conversation my family had years ago, just after my grandfather's funeral. We were talking about him, and how he had been divorced from my grandmother 30 years before. My aunt had brought up how hard he was to live with, how poorly he'd treated my grandmother. My uncle added "He'd do anything just to aggravate her. Whatever she wanted, he purposely did the exact opposite." How sad. How can you live with someone you know is always trying to aggravate you? You don't. And ultimately she didn't.

Some men too just have no manners. It goes beyond the routine tribulations of romantic relationships. He hurt our feelings but didn't mean to. It's more like they consistently fail to follow the medical credo – first do no harm. First treat people like fellow human beings, the golden rule and all that. I know so many women who do not even get human decency from the men they are dating. They stand them up. They don't call, they don't pay for things, they don't pay back money (what are you doing with someone who borrows money in the first place?). They move on to another woman without bothering to say anything. Any similar action in the business world would severely impact their success. Ruin their career. Why is it okay for men to do these things with someone they claim to care about? They say all is fair in love and war, but it shouldn't have to be that awful.

There are conditions like these that are garden variety nastiness and there are other, more entrenched personality issues to consider in picking or sticking with a man.

One reason why some men are so difficult is because they have ADD, Attention Deficit Disorder. Go ahead, laugh. But this condition might cause more relationship problems than any other. A man with ADD is disorganized. He gets overwhelmed easily. He's often late. He's distracted all the time. He loses stuff. He gets angry when he's pressured. He forgets things you tell him. He doesn't listen well. He interrupts you. He blurts things out and has no filter.

When I was in graduate school in the early 90s, this disorder was just gaining scholarly interest. I was studying adult learning, and I came across the concept, so I did some research and wrote a paper about it. At the time, ADD seemed like a bit of a crock, like doesn't everyone have this? We're all too busy. Distracted. Get overwhelmed. But since then, the disorder has gotten a lot more scholarly attention and credibility.

Ian, my last relationship, had been diagnosed with ADD, and because of it, being with him was a constant challenge. In addition to the constant lateness, losing stuff, and interrupting, he would get overwhelmed easily and just shut down. If there were multiple things going on- dinner cooking, the phone ringing, we needed to be somewhere soon- I would wonder if he was going to stop talking for several hours, or go hide in the bedroom, all things he had done before. Whether it was all ADD or not, he also had no filter, and was known to blurt things out without stopping to consider how he was delivering the message. A verbal compulsion of sorts. I knew he loved me, and he didn't mean to be hurtful, but I still got tired of having to constantly be patient and understanding when in fact I was often hurt or pissed off.

Like any disability, I don't think having ADD exempts someone from responsibility for their actions. But when someone's brain functions a certain way, there isn't much you can do about it but manage the symptoms. And there are pharmaceutical and behavioral ways to do that.

So I'm not saying if he has ADD, run. Maybe you have ADD. But far more men than women do, and it can be hard on relationships. So just think about it. Those behaviors which are incredibly alienating and make him seem socially inept may in fact be part of a larger issue. If you suspect he has ADD, learn about it. For more information, look online, or see the work of Edward Hallowell and others. They all suggest strategies that help, like scheduling your weekly and monthly activities, doing less, setting boundaries around when you talk about relationship or household issues. Try some of the tips and see if it becomes more manageable. Encourage him to get diagnosed if you suspect ADD, and even for him to consider taking medication. Many people have, and from what I've seen, it makes a huge difference. In my relationship with Ian, it wasn't the ADD that ultimately broke us up, but it was a factor. We had to manage it constantly. While we were together, we agreed to certain strategies. We both made sure not to book too many things. He tried to stop himself before saying something uncouth. I would put my hand up to keep him from interrupting me. He would tell me if he was feeling overwhelmed and needed quiet, before he shut down and didn't talk at all. Sound like a lot? It was. But only I could decide if it is worth it to me. If the good outweighed the bad.

Disorder or no, men generally can't multitask. It's basic neurobiology. They think with one side of the brain at a time. Either left or right. Women think in circular brain patterns, so we're able to be right brained, creative, and left brained, analytical, at the same time. Trace it to its biological origins. Caring for children while gathering roots and sticks and trying to avoid getting eaten by a saber-toothed tiger. We likely evolved to be able to manage multiple demands on our attention. Men likely got to be single-minded of purpose. Hunting for dinner. So we have to be kind to men on this one. When it gets down to a "can't do" or a "won't do", sometimes they just can't.

Another reason why? Because he's a narcissist. He has a serious personality disorder. Something is warped in there. Narcissists are characterized by several things, but central to their makeup is a profound lack of empathy. They are not able to feel the experience of other people, or see how their actions affect them. And they don't care to either. Many of them are cheaters, because they don't connect to how that hurts their partner, and they never get enough attention and energy, so one woman will not be enough. They always need more.

A narcissist is typically very charming, and he will often be the nicest person you know to children and strangers. Then he'll make the most cutting remark to you, something like "Don't you ever shut up?"

I consider my ex David, the labor lawyer, to be a narcissist. I remember many times when he would leave me somewhere because he got angry at me, for what I could never recall. Whenever I tried to end the relationship, break free from the emotional abuse, he would come in at the 11th hour and tell me he much he loved me. I remember the night I replied "You keep telling me you love me, but I don't *feel* like you love me." I didn't feel cared for, considered, appreciated. His response? "I hate when you get emotional like this. You become so ugly." Nice, huh?

Narcissists also lie about their abilities or credentials. They fake things to impress people, or get sympathy. Narcissists don't feel adequate deep down, and they will say anything to feel better about themselves. Chronic lying stems from self-hatred. I've listened to many women talk about lies men have told them- that there was no one else, that they had plenty of money in the bank, lies about where they went to school, what they did for a living. Then of course there are those men you hear about who are married to multiple women. They say they are traveling for business, but they are carrying on separate lives, raising multiple families, and the women never knew about it. Those men are definitely narcissists.

When you meet him, the narcissist usually seems too good to be true. He pushes commitment too soon. He'll say "I love you" at three weeks. "Let's move in together" at two months. You are completely idealized. Never has a woman been so beautiful, so caring, such a good lover, and so meant for him. He feels blessed to have found you, and this confirms everything you've ever secretly hoped about yourself. That you are that gorgeous, smart and wonderful creature. You are, by the way. But you didn't dare hope to find a man to say it, and so soon!

But then they disappear, leaving you in their wake.

Probably the worst part about being involved with a narcissist is the way they idealize, then discard you. It is a common occurrence. The literature on the subject is fascinating - they quite literally turn off you. They are done sucking up the energy you have to offer, and they are not interested any more. The things he used to find charming about you now are repulsive. And you are usually devastated. What happened? What did I do? Where did he go?

You didn't do anything. He was just done with you.

This personality disorder is almost impossible to change. Narcissists are so ego-driven- they don't think anything is wrong with them. All their actions are justifiable. They rarely respond to therapy. People change when the pain of staying the same gets too great. These guys are never in pain. They always find a new mirror in which to gaze upon themselves. To change, you have to think you should. They don't.

Why else? Because some men are misogynists. They hate women. Like a narcissist, a misogynist is good at hiding who he is. Someone who hates women usually won't come out and say it. What he will say is that he hates his mother. Or that his ex-wife is a bitch. Or that some woman he works with is a man-hating dyke. Granted, some women are worthy of scorn. But the misogynist has a far more deep seated anger. And he will take it out on you at some point. Curt remarks, passive/aggressive actions, even violence. All designed to bring you down.

Long ago I realized that someone doesn't have to whack you across the face to be abusing you.

A former colleague of mine is a reformed Don Juan. He battled cancer in his 40s; he finally got married for the first time in his early 50s. Now he stays on the straight and narrow. But for many years, he was a cad. A big one. Seeing five women at once, some in different states, some in his hometown, some at work. He used to run personal ads with the heading "Lonely Millionaire".

Years ago, we were driving to a meeting one afternoon, and had spent the drive talking about Bill Clinton and Monica Lewinsky, which was all over the news at the time. I asked this reformed womanizer "Why do men do it? Why do they lie and cheat?" His response was swift "Many men hate women. Period. They justify their behavior by saying she's stupid, she should have seen it coming." There it was. On the ride back to our office, a woman in the car in front of us was hesitating to turn left. This was taking about five seconds, but he was getting impatient. "That's it sweetie", he said sarcastically, "you take your sweet little time. Maybe file your nails first." A shiver went up my spine. Not so reformed after all.

How can you detect these guys? Often you can't right away. But just like a narcissist, there will be some clues. They don't like their mother. They don't get along with women at work. They say denigrating things to and about women. They talk to women like they are stupid. They call them derogatory names. One friend briefly dated a guy who liked to rant at the women on TV, if you can get that. Particularly on shows like Jerry Springer or Oprah. He'd say things like "you stupid slut, what a dumb broad, etc." Great. Class all the way. It didn't take long for her to GET OUT. And what finally did it was while watching TV one night, she made a comment about the program, and he turned to her and asked "Don't you have an off button?" Bingo. Time to turn him off.

Cherchez la Mere

This is French for "find the mother." I know I don't need to say this to you, but when you get involved with a man, immediately look at how he treats his mother. What he says about her, how often he sees her. And ditto for the sisters. Many a man may be nice to his mother- certainly doesn't come out and say he hates her. But he acts like she's a pain in the ass, or resents even the mildest demands she puts on him. This is the model he grew up with; his relationship with his mother formed how he relates to women. Even far more than what a daughter learns from her father. Because typically the mother is the primary caregiver, at least she was for men of older generations. She was the one who doled out praise or scorn. She was the one he likely feared. His mother had a lot of power over him.

Also ask him about how his father treated his mother. There are numerous studies on abuse that address how when a father is abusive, it is often the son who steps in to protect his mother. This experience might have taught him that women are weak and need to be protected. Or that abuse is a legitimate way for a man to control a woman.

It goes the other way too. Two long term partners in my life were raised by mothers who were incredibly caring and loving. Too much. These men were doted on, praised, given money, given emotional support no matter what lame brained schemes or messes they got themselves into. And these men ended up being great about gender issues, very respectful of women. Women in the workplace, gender equality, sharing the housework. But they also ended up being emotional cripples of a sort. They were still getting money from Mom in their 40s, a time when they should have been supporting their parents, not the other way around. And both were very self-absorbed. They were used to being catered to, and thinking of others and their needs did not come naturally or easily. They also had huge issues with engulfment- they were afraid to get emotionally close for fear of being smothered, like they were by Mom.

Like narcissists, misogynists often are attracted to strong women who are successful, independent and responsible. And thus more likely to take criticism and try to improve. Strong, smart women are the big game. It's far more pleasurable to take a woman like this down than it is one who's meek and subservient to begin with.

I have experienced this misogynist phenomena firsthand. The little jokes, sarcastic comments, barbs. One guy I briefly dated was a successful business consultant and writer. We had a lot in common, did the same kind of work. We started off slow, and he was complimentary about my confidence and sense of self, saying to me on our first date "there aren't many women like you." True that! I felt comfortable with him, like he wouldn't be threatened by my accomplishments. But after dating a few weeks, he began to criticize me. I took him to a function at the university I teach at; afterward he told me I was too aggressive with the Dean, and that I was flirting with a male colleague. Then a few weeks later, he made a joke about my height and weight, my being bigger than he was. Then there was a joke about how "verbal" I was. A joke that really was more like "don't you ever shut up?"

The bell went off. I've been in this movie before.

On a far lesser note, I have read and observed how often men act badly to test you, or to drive you away. The testing part we can almost overlook. He wants to know the boundaries, he wants to know you care. So if he makes an off remark, or goes out too long with the boys, you put him in his place. It's annoying, but so long as it is not overly disrespectful, it's relatively harmless. Just a little boundary testing.

Maybe. But here you must go into observation mode. Does he keep doing it? What is it about? How bad does it make you feel? Do you have that sinking suspicion that he's saying it to control you? My ex Ian had this passive aggressive trick he'd pull every time we'd have a discussion about the relationship. He'd listen to me, give his input, agree to change something or step up in some way. We'd resolved it. Then, he would be too busy to see me for a week. Or he wouldn't call that night, or the next. It was like clockwork. It was like he was saying "ok, you get what you want, but I'm still going to get my freedom." Psychological freedom is what we seek when someone gives us a "no". We need to feel like we are still in control. So we find some escape hatch. Now this isn't necessarily unhealthy when it's about your diet, or even your work, something that doesn't negatively impact other people. We all act out to release emotions. But to do it in a romantic relationship is immature. Grow up. What's this man going to do when you have to deal with something serious? Like you're diagnosed with cancer and he has to skip going to the gym so he can take you to chemo? Is he going to punish you for that?

This type of man operates from the premise that the best defense is a good offense. Maybe you're upset with him about something. Or maybe you've done something to displease him. Rather than sit you down and say to you "listen, this is what I've observed..." and go from there, he's just going to make you feel bad until you stop doing, saying or feeling what it is that he doesn't like.

When you stick up for yourself, a response you often get from these men is what I like to call "in fairness to me." You bring up an issue in the relationship, either big or small, and rather than being met with concern and care – "oh, honey, how can we work this out?"- they meet you with something like "well, in fairness to me, you talk about your ex-boyfriend too,"or "I may have been late to your mother's, but you've been late before too." They are, again, putting you on the defensive to avoid taking any responsibility for their own actions.

Fairness is a value that everyone shares. No one likes to be on the receiving end of injustice. Everyone likes to think that they are fair to other people as well, that they are never unjust. In the end, we also want to believe that life is fair. Who wants to think of a world where bad deeds go unpunished and good deeds unrewarded?

So fairness is a universal value. When you are met with, "well, *you're* unfair," a woman will usually take responsibility for it. Maybe she wasn't aware she was doing something so inconsiderate. She'll apologize maybe, or mull it over. It's hard to counter this argument from a man- "in fairness to me." And men know it. Many men don't have the maturity to say "I'm sorry. How can I fix it?" So they take the power position, which is to make her feel bad, make her fix it, even though it was her rightful complaint in the first place.

Nowhere is this more evident than in a breakup. When some men want to break up with you they'll just act like jerks for a while until you get frustrated with them and break it off yourself. Highly annoying and highly immature. Why can't they just say it? Are they so afraid of female anger and wrath that they'll avoid it at any costs? Yes. I think it is all about the mother, again, as she was the primary care giver and the one who determined their fate. As children they learned to fear female wrath. They know you're going to be angry, and they don't want to be punished.

In the end, men don't care who leaves who like we do. It's not an ego thing like it is for us. We make sure to say "**I** broke up with **him**!" Men just want to get out so they often try to get you to break up with them. They keep upping the ante so that any woman with a shred of self respect would have to bail on them first.

It's like at work when a manager treats an employee so badly-moves their desk to outside the bathroom, takes away their staff, refuses to look at them, just so they'll quit. Hey, the company pays unemployment either way. And meanwhile, you're risking a lawsuit. And it's just so cowardly.

In a very *Sex and the City* move a client of mine was dumped via a Hallmark card the night before Valentine's Day. She had been dating a doctor, an older man. She'd had reservations about the age difference (20 years) but he'd been warm, funny, sophisticated in ways the younger men she'd dated were not. It was only two months of dating, but a good two months. Lots of kissing and conversations deep into the night. So she expected they'd have a good holiday, even though he had yet to make plans with her. She checked her mailbox the night before Valentines Day and found a card from him, in a pink envelope with hearts on it. She opened it expecting a statement of affection. Instead it read "I have run into an old flame and want to pursue this relationship now but have so enjoyed our time together….." Honestly. A short phone call was too much to ask, given that they live in a small community and are sure to run into each other? He's a physician; he's used to giving bad news. You have cancer. You need a triple bypass. He can't pick up the phone and just say it?

Why?

Because at the end of the day, you still can't make a silk purse out of a sow's ear.

Who's Got the Power?

I've always liked that 90's song "I Got the Power." Every time I'd hear it, I'd think, oh really? We never know who has the power in a relationship. Because it shifts on a continual basis, whoever has it now may not tomorrow. Sometimes power in a relationship is about "the power of the least interested." The partner who could more easily let go has the upper hand.

People don't like to talk about power, either at work, like the position power that comes from having a certain job title or connections, or in their personal lives, like the power we have over our families. But power plays exist everywhere. Other people have power over us when we give it to them.

Take the relationship of a much older man with a much younger woman. The legendary May-December trading of wealth for beauty. Who is getting the better deal? The woman gets access to money, provided the economy and the stock portfolio are solid. The man gets the youngest and sleekest model, forgetting or not caring that they are far less likely to have anything in common. What's even worse to me though are the men in their 40s and 50s, never married, having made money all their lives, who now want to meet a woman in her 20s or 30s and have children. They will not date a woman their own age. Yes, these men want kids, but many women can conceive later in life, and there's surrogates, adoption, blended families. I've met many men in this age bracket who will not even *consider* a woman their own age. He has the power to choose only much younger women. But I figure a guy who's 49, 53, 57, maybe has 20-25 years left to live. And they ain't the good years either. In a few years his much younger wife is going to be changing his diapers along with their kids. And he's going to widow her when she's in her 50s and faces some tough competition from younger women. So not the best setup.

I admit I don't respect those huge age differences. I know love knows no age, and I shouldn't be so judgmental, but I don't like it for women either. I'm going to date some hot 25 year old? Great. Till we try to have a conversation about the economy or I get jealous when he flirts with women his own age.

Society continually stresses to women that your power is in your looks, and once you start aging, you're doomed. So make sure you don't look like you're aging. And do your best to dress and act like younger women, who are all competition for you in an odds-against-you fight.

Another element of power- and one that puts women in a horrible position-is that sometimes you only have the power when they are wanting you. Once you give in, the tables often turn. We all know that before sex, women are thinking clearly. Men aren't. After sex, it reverses. It's not only in sex though that we see this. Many men dig you when you ignore them. They will pursue and pursue if even if there is no hope it will connect. Just like when you're dating, you pull back, they come forward. It's a classic psychological model called pursuer/distancer. It is aggravating but it can be used to your advantage.

I don't mean what most people think – the classic hard to get. I don't like that. That is a game, a manipulation, and one you can't keep up. I am more advocating the power of the least interested. You enjoy his company, he's fun, and as long as he's not difficult, you will keep him around. Even if he is your husband. You may be his wife, but at any given time, you are your own woman. Yes, you want love, connection and intimacy. But you aren't going to sell your soul for it. Because men are hunters, as we always hear, the "old shoe" girlfriend or wife can lose appeal over time. So sometimes you need to step back. Be less predictable. Let him wonder where you are. Don't pick up every time he calls. Don't always tell him everything you're doing. As Sherri Argov says in *Why Men Love Bitches* "Men don't respond to words. Men respond to no contact."

There is a way to be in love with a man, but in love with yourself more. You can hold both places in the world, with effort. Women want the abandon of love, the "he is the one and I'm the happiest girl in the world" feeling. If we get it, we want it to last. We want to lock it down. He's mine. And we think a committed relationship will solve all our doubts and struggles. But it doesn't. When you are committed to yourself, the best path for you, your circumstances may change. And who you become may not be right for him. Or his emotional changes right for you. We all should have the personal power to walk when a situation no longer suits us.

Also, as I have heartbreakingly found, sometimes love is not enough. You can love him and he you, but there are things that are non-negotiable. Dealbreakers. Like he doesn't want children, and you do. Or he has an addiction and it continues to wreak havoc on your mental health and finances. Only you can decide what is too much to compromise on. And when you need to fold 'em and walk away.

On the harsher note, if you are looking for love, sometimes your best bet lies in being ambivalent. One of my funniest lessons in this stuff happened when I was a freshman in high school. It was at a school dance. I was in a little posse of girls, and one of them had just been dumped by her cruel senior boyfriend. We all herded in to the girl's room to process. As we came in, we saw this older girl slouched against the sinks, wearing black, smoking a cigarette and looking eerily like Joan Jett. We gave her a glance of apprehension then crowded around the sinks to comfort our sobbing friend. *He's such an asshole. Oh you poor thing. He'll come back don't worry.* The older girl started laughing at us. "Hey," she called out, taking a drag. "Let me give you girls a little advice. You have to learn to fuck 'em and chuck 'em." The posse gasped, the dumped started sobbing harder, and

I just nodded, like wow, yeah, cool. That's how you do it. I never forgot that.

Easier said than done. Sure. And we do not like to think of ourselves as users, or goldiggers. Or sluts for that matter. I don't mean it that way. I mean it in terms that men use. A man doesn't keep calling unless he's getting something out of it. And most men, when they are not, will move on. When they call a woman, they are not likely thinking "is she the one?" or "how should I play this?" They are most likely thinking she seems like fun, how long will it take me to sleep with her?

We have to find a way to keep that power of ambivalence after we sleep with a man, rather than imbuing him with properties he doesn't deserve. He must be a nice guy because we already slept with him. Hey, this may or may not be the guy. You'll let him know. Meanwhile, your mission is to take care of you. To have the courage and commitment to do what's right for you, even when it's hard or it hurts. Not to hold the actress Alicia Silverstone up as some paragon of female power, but I read an interview with her in a women's magazine years ago. She was talking about going with your inner wisdom. I cut out one quote and keep it on my fridge. She said "Becoming a woman is feeling an enormous sense of self worth and self confidence. And listening to my gut. Your gut really speaks loud and clear. Rather than trying to figure out, is it me or is it them? It's "this is just making me uncomfortable." Leave! You stop trying to blame yourself or overanalyze it. It's just "no."

I always tell women I counsel- if you know he is the one, then fight for him. Do what it takes to work through your differences. Be as patient as you can with his fear of commitment, if that's the issue, and it often is. I say this because YOU chose. Not him. You are not running a popularity contest for his attention. He may or may not agree that you two are meant to be. And if he doesn't, then he isn't the one. But in the interim, you know what YOU want, and therefore you are far more likely to get it. That is called agency. The ability to act well on your own behalf.

It is imperative not to give your power away. No man is the end all and be all of your existence. He is not the one for you if he is being an ass. As painful as it may be, it's always better to know this sooner than later when you are further in. Men can love you one moment and are making plans, then the next they tell you they are going back to an ex-girlfriend, or that you two "aren't connecting." But men are also like buses, another one comes along every 15 minutes. There will be a day when one stays, and you want him to stay. And you will look at all the others you wasted time and energy on and say "I can't believe that seemed like such a big deal at the time. That I had so much grief over him when he wasn't right for me."

I love that joke "How long does it take a woman to get over a breakup? Who says she does?" Funny, but we need to change that. We hold onto heartache far too long, and we keep ourselves from letting go and moving on.

I mentioned I've been studying Buddhism for a few years now. I don't have the patience or the energy to become a Buddhist. I just get a lot out of the teachings, and try to employ the easier principles. Compassion. Patience. Detachment. Elimination of desire. We all know stuff doesn't make us happy. We're not going to be happy when we get a bigger house, or a boat, or a new car. Even losing weight or getting a great man won't do it. Suffering comes from always being unsatisfied and thinking someone else has it better than we do.

It's like women who are incredibly attractive. We think the world must be their oyster, that they get to have the finest experiences in life. I read in *Self* magazine once that 80% of American women think their lives would be better if they were thinner. Of course, it's not true. We have all lost those 10-20 pounds (and regained them) and found our lives were just the same! Maybe worse because we felt we *should* be happier. The mild obsessive compulsive disorder it takes to stay thinner than your body wants takes energy and joy away from other pursuits. Also, women who are gorgeous aren't any more likely to get a man. In fact it can be harder for good looking women to find men who are not intimidated by them, and who are equally attractive. Or not shallow and just into her for her looks. Michelle Pfeiffer once said in an *Allure* article that beautiful women get used all the time. Men know they may be a slave to their vanity; they are used to getting positive strokes from men. And men can manipulate them with that. It can be a burden just as easily as it is a joy.

Yes, it helps to be attractive. You probably get admiring glances. You're better able to compete in the open market. You may even develop higher self esteem, because people treat you better. But despite these perks, you are basically still you. You stay the same. So power, and agency, come from within. If you want to change something in your life, you know you can still do it even with those extra 20 pounds.

I never knew the achievements I was going to have to work hardest for in life were the emotional ones. We are always told that life requires hard work; success demands it. It's an American ideal. We get that we have to put in long hours at work and schmooze and work our butts off. We get the concept of face time, being there, anywhere and everywhere- the office, the gym, at church, in the classroom, at home with your kids. Yet I now see that the most difficult situations in my life weren't about externals, but were about me. My perspective. We can be our own worst enemies sometimes. Wasting time on ill-suited men, hyper-stress jobs, frustrating friendships. When I was diagnosed with cancer, I thought about all those difficult relationships in my past, and I wanted that time back. Two years with David. One year with Nick. Etc. I couldn't get it of course, yet out of that feeling, I learned to continually consider situations from the perspective of "What is good for me?" and "Is this what I want?

When relationships end, we must see it as part of the natural order, and not blame ourselves. Endings are hard, and if you're not careful, you can get stuck in mental traps, like thinking if you were prettier he would have loved you more. Or if he cheated on you, that you should have seen it. Or predicted it, because he's cheated on other partners. Maybe. People do show us who they are, we just refuse to pay attention. But I am tired of blaming the victim. Naiveté gets punished enough on its own. Let's blame the person who did the damage. That seems fairer. We seem to be living in a society where people do not take personal responsibility. So let's start making them.

So say it with me. He is the last asshole. Remember that movie with Bruce Willis, *The Last Boy Scout*? Well, if you are unloading a bad man, that man is the last asshole. Take a stand. You deserve better and the only way you're going to get it is by fighting for yourself. Moving on. Waiting and working for something better. Put all that energy you've put into trying to get along with him into yourself and you will see a change. The same goes for if you are married to him. The sooner you get out, the sooner you can rebuild your life and meet the right man. I know it is hard. I know. I know. But it's hard staying too. And don't forget the universe loves a vacuum. If there is no room in your life, how can the right thing come into it? Do not live in fear. Believe in the law of attraction, in bringing the good things to yourself.

Besides, you're never more gorgeous than when you're walking out the door.

Paris Syndrome

They get what they want and they never want it again...

– Courtney Love, Hole

Years ago, my close friend Ann began seeing a guy she'd once dated in college. Now they were in their early 30s, and the relationship was going great. She thought maybe reuniting after all these years meant he was the one.

They'd been dating about four months when one night he told Ann he loved her. She was ecstatic, because she'd fallen in love too. Then a few days after that he said "Let's go to Paris for a long weekend. I'll buy the tickets. Just a few days. To celebrate." She was delighted! He said he'd arrange everything.

Three days later rather than showing her the itinerary, he broke up with her. She was shocked and horribly upset, then demanded to know why. "But you just asked me to go to Paris!" she exclaimed. He shrugged and said "Well, I really wanted to go with you when I asked you."

Hence the birth of Paris Syndrome.

The phenomenon where men say one thing one minute or day or month, and something entirely different the next. It is miraculously forgotten. Because maybe it wasn't felt much to begin with.

Sometimes it's small in scope. A man calls, asking "What are you doing Friday night?"

You answer "I don't have definite plans, what's up?"

He says "Great. Let's get together. I'll call you Thursday night to pick a time and place."

Thursday comes, no call.

This is frustrating and disappointing. But it's a scary world when you can be with someone for a while, and you have that conversation where he says "I love you. I'm so glad I met you." And the next day he breaks up with you because "things haven't been good for some time." Huh? Or you think you're happily married and you find out your husband is cheating, or you're married to a man who always said he wanted kids, and now that you're trying to conceive he decides it really isn't for him.

Huh?

My own experiences with Paris Syndrome are far more than I'd like to recall. But one relationship comes to mind. It is the relationship that more than any other drove me to write this book.

My ex-boyfriend Nick broke up with me not once, but four times. Looking back on it, I cringe. I kept letting him back in my life, my heart, my bed. For a whole year we went back and forth. That's how long it took me to be able to let him go.

We had met years before we dated. Whenever I'd run into him, we'd have great conversations, but one of us was always dating someone else. When we finally connected, I was six months out of a relationship I had ended. He was two months out of one where she went back to her ex-husband and informed him at the last minute. He wasn't in great shape.

I knew this, but we talked about it, and he assured me he was ready to start a new relationship.

Fast forward several months to breakup one. His ex-girlfriend had been calling him, showing up where she knew he'd be. She didn't want him back but she didn't want to let go either. It was upsetting to me, but we were doing great-my son liked him. I was growing close to his teenage daughter. My friends and family liked him. There was promise and I didn't want to give up too soon. He felt overwhelmed, thought maybe he needed a little more time after all. We agreed to a break for him to clear his head.

We reconnected a week later, amid declarations of "I missed you. I can't be without you." We then had a few more good months, amid discussions of moving in together and helping raise each other's children. He even proposed at one point. I said it was way too soon, but I could see it happening someday.

Then one night, we went out to dinner with another couple. We had been arguing earlier, because he was late to meet us and didn't call, but over our chicken marsalas, he took my hand and whispered in my ear "You're the one for me. I want to be with you forever." Two hours later, back at my house, he hugged me, sighed over my shoulder and whispered "This just isn't going to work."

Huh?

A few months go by. A few sad, hard months. Yes, he was wishy-washy, unreliable. But the good things were so good. I missed him. Then I saw him out one night. We talked, made plans to get together. Started hanging out again, went out with those couple friends, went away for a weekend. He told me he was "working on his issues," and seemed to have made some big changes. A new job, a new house, the ex-girlfriend had moved to Florida. Things carry on for another month then he bails again.

Four more months go by. Then one average April afternoon, I got diagnosed with cancer. Nick was the least of my concerns at that point, but he heard about it from mutual friends, sought me out. Offered compassion and concern. We got involved again. Three more months together. Helpful months. I was scared; he was comforting. When your hair is falling out and your skin puffing up and the man who gave you the best sex of your life wants to help you through it, you take it. I used to joke with him after we'd make love. "Me and my immune system thank you," I'd say, running a puffy hand across his chest hair.

You know where this is going, right?

Then poof, one night he didn't show up for dinner as planned. I kept calling his cell, thinking he was dead at the side of the road. You'd think I'd have gotten it by now.

When he finally did call back, at midnight, in a sheepish voice he said "I don't know what to say."

I said "I do. Goodbye." And I hung up.

I have never talked to him again. That was five years ago.

Now I forgive myself for putting up with this back and forth (see the chapter on women and self esteem) because there were qualities about him that I really appreciated – his sense of humor, his politics, his adventurous spirit- ok, he was *great* in bed. By Round Three, I suppose I had given up much hope of him as a permanent partner. But I still felt a little glimmer. He seemed to be making progress. Every partner you meet will have certain liabilities you'll have to accommodate. I was still figuring out if his was too much.

The worst part of his indecision though was that all through this, I took him at his word. I expected him to be honest. If he didn't want to be with me, he'd tell me, right? Why would a man say things he didn't mean?

While women certainly do lie, studies will tell you that most women's lies tend to be social courtesy lies. "No, you don't look fat in those pants." "Sorry, I can't make it to your dog's birthday party because I have to take my mother to the doctor." Chances are if a woman said something at 9:00 PM one night, she's still going to mean it the next night at 9:00 PM.

Men on the other hand seem to lie more frequently than we do, and have lies with greater scope. "Honey, she is just a friend" comes to mind. Or Bernie Madoff saying he's made you all this money. Tiger Woods saying to a woman "You're the only one." If you want to read a very scary book, read *101 Lies Men tell Women*. You may never trust again.

If Nick were an isolated incident, I wouldn't be writing this chapter. But he's not. They may say women are fickle, but my observations are that men are far more so. There is a fickle nature to their attraction to us. Sometimes they're into you, sometimes not. Sometimes they appreciate all those things that are great about you – your intelligence, warmth, humor. You start to relax and enjoy yourself. But then you start to notice he isn't calling as much. Or doesn't seem as excited to see you. Many married women complain that their husbands are distant, seem to have lost interest in them, stop spending time with them, stop initiating sex.

Paris Syndrome is inherently about the difference in how men and women care. Over the years, I've listened to so many women hurt by the lack of caring shown by men who have professed to love them. I have had 20 years of male students, 30 years of working with men. The level of self-absorption in many men can be stunning. They do what they want to do. It's how they were raised in their homes and socialized in the world.

I'm not talking about the basic level of psychological freedom. I mean more that feeling so many of us get that he just, for lack of a better term, doesn't give a shit. He doesn't *care* about you.

For years I told my husband I wanted to leave the Midwest, and for years I felt like he didn't care. His career was going well, he wanted to stay. When I'd complain, I'd get retorts like "You didn't give up much leaving the Northeast- a junk job, a clinging family," to just humoring me about applying for jobs back home, to coldly reminding me I said I'd wait for five years, till he got tenure. I didn't feel the comfort of "I know this is hard, we're in this together" and I grew more and more resentful. Over the years it soured me on him and the marriage.

Personally, I have always attracted self-absorbed men. For several reasons. I grew up in a family where people were pretty remote and emotionally unavailable. I'm comfortable with it, even if it's not healthy. It feels normal. I'm also very independent. I never give up going out with the girls on a weekend or seeing male friends for a beer, just because I have a boyfriend. A lot of men wouldn't be comfortable with that. The self absorbed guy is, because it means you'll leave him alone and won't bug him about spending so much time away from you on *his* interests. I also like intellectual guys; I need someone smart and well read. I've found these types of men are more likely to be consumed with themselves. Their interests, ideas, goals. Not to globalize, but as an academic myself, there is a high likelihood you're enamored with your own viewpoints. You have to be to get up in front of strangers and sell your view of the world all day long.

I accept that I will probably always attract and be attracted to men like this. I also know it's what I do about it that makes a difference.

One way to combat Paris Syndrome is to observe if this man is someone who keeps his word in all areas of his life. Does he let down his boss? His friends? His family? Are there inconsistencies in the information he shares with people? As you observe things in a man you don't like or respect, be willing to act on it too. Just don't say "Oh, I'm lonely and this seems like fun." Think you know, I've been here before and when it bites the dust it hurts. I love myself too much to waste my time. So if you see red flags? That red flag means **stop**, not **charge**.

As I said earlier, and as Oprah often says, people show us who they are, we just choose not to listen. Men show us who they are the first time we meet them. With online dating, sometimes they show us before we meet, in an email or a phone call. Did he say his ex-wife was a bitch? Or maybe he said his phone was shut off or credit card declined. Maybe you meet him at a party- while he's talking to you is he giving a sideways glance to the busty blonde over by the onion dip? Maybe he's not Mr. Loyal. How is he dressed? Shallow, maybe, but wrinkled, ripped clothes or perfectly pressed Dockers speak volumes.

Treat the process of getting involved like you would moving for a new job or hiring someone to work for you. Get information. Ask around. Google him. Run a criminal record check even. Above all, do your homework.

You must also observe how a man treats himself, because people who don't treat themselves well don't usually treat others well. Does he eat well? Exercise? Pay his bills on time? Keep in touch with his mother? Attend family functions? Nick did none of these things. It was a strong sign of his character, but I chose to ignore it at my peril.

The best posture to take with a man is what a therapist friend of mine calls "gathering information." You are observing, looking for indicators of his character so you can make an informed decision about whether you want to get involved with him. This takes time. But what's your rush? Women often get emotionally involved with a guy too quickly, then immediately start tweaking on "Is he the guy?" and "Where is this going?" and "What's going to happen?" We are getting way ahead of ourselves here. Don't rush to judgment or even the "need to know." Just sit back and take a posture of gathering information.

Starting a new relationship can certainly stir your fears and anxieties. It is hard to let go of the programming of past hurts, and when you are stressed, they often rear their ugly head in thoughts like "Oh, I can't get hurt again!" or "Oh, this is what happened last time!" The brain loves patterns to order and manage the world around you; it will seek them every time. "Gerry is just like Paul, and he left me, and I didn't see it, and this happened last time and it sucked, and it's going to happen now....." You can drive yourself crazy with this stuff. That happened then. This is now. It's just your desire for control talking. You want to know what's going to happen.

In your state of not-knowingness, you must keep an open heart and an open mind. You can't be ready for love if your heart and mind are closed, and if you're just awaiting your next disappointment. You will not bring the right man to you unless you have an open heart to receive him. And it will be hard to keep him if you keep operating from the same old fears and anxieties, if you don't have also have an open mind to accept him as he is.

Let your past hurts go, and while you're at it, don't beat yourself up when you're wrong about a man in the future. We women love to take the blame on ourselves. *I should have seen*, or *I should have known*. Maybe, maybe not. But either way, so what? Dust yourself off and do better next time. Learning is a lifelong process. When we are ready for the lesson, the teacher appears. He was your teacher. You got something out of him. Whether you spent ten years together, or just ten days.

Sometimes you are in a place where you couldn't have avoided a bad man any more than you could avoid any other natural disaster, like a tornado or a flood. He was a false prince. He seemed like the Prince Charming you were waiting for, but he wasn't the guy. Accepting impermanence also means that you accept that a man may be right for a certain time in your life, but it might just fall apart one day. And not because you were doing anything wrong. If it does bite the dust, learn how to get over it quicker. It doesn't have to take forever. Enjoy the things you did get out of it. I have had some very romantic times in my life. Dancing in the streets of Vienna to usher in the new year. Sailing along the New England coast, drinking champagne and watching the sunset over the water. Long motorcycle rides through lush Iowa cornfields. Herding sheep and counting rainbows in the Irish countryside. All of these experiences were ones I wanted to continue. But the relationships didn't, for various reasons. But I am still very thankful to have had these experiences. They have shaped my life. And without these false princes, these things wouldn't have happened.

Yeah, I only feel so thankful on good days. On off days, I can grow melancholy for those experiences I'd like to have again. The good days are getting more frequent, though, because I refuse to sit around and think love isn't going to come my way. I believe it will. In the meantime, I'm going to live a great life.

I try to use my experiences as lessons in learning how to enjoy the present, and not obsess about the future. How do you do that? Don't overinvest for one. Try to keep your expectations in check. Try to take your time with the physical stuff too. It helps. Because then you keep your clarity a little longer. You can really know who this guy is before the bonding hormones, oxytocin and dopamine, kick in. Making you imbue a man with properties he doesn't deserve. Like he must be a great guy if I slept with him.

Adopt a mindset of constant quality improvement too. How many writers, artists and actors went through years of rejection before they hit it big? Years of odd jobs and family disapproval, where only their tenacity kept them going? Victor Frankel in his book *Man's Search for Meaning* recounts how the only people who survived the concentration camps were those determined to fight to survive, who refused to give in to the cruelty, death and despair they saw around them. Those who lost that will died quickly.

I've had no greater example of this than when I was in central Europe last summer. I was struck by the history of Poland in particular. This is a country that didn't exist for large periods of time. It was always being swallowed up by Germany, Russia or Austria, its more powerful neighbors. At different times, its citizens were forbidden from speaking Polish or calling themselves Poles. After

WWII, when millions of Poles had been murdered in concentration camps, the Soviets came in and put the country under 40 years of Communist rule. Off and on, Poles suffered centuries of oppression. But like many other war-torn places, Poland survived, and today they have a growing economy.

These may seem like extreme examples. But they are powerful reminders to me when I'm down about my love life. Humans are resilient. People have survived far worse despair than I have in my search for love.

In any meaningful pursuit, what choice is there but to persevere?

Islands in the Stream

Here is the single woman's dilemma. What do you do when you are waiting for Mr. Right? Do you just sit at home, staying celibate, and pray that he comes along soon? Or do you only last so long, because you really miss affection and sex, and decide to engage with a few Mr. Right Nows? I can go without for long stretches of time, not happily, but not crazily. I just get busy with hobbies, traveling, going out with girlfriends, etc. But if it will be years before I meet the right one, I'd like to have a little island in the stream, a little shelter from the storm.

Who is such a person you may ask? In my not extensive research, I have observed that the island in the stream, (or f-buddy, or friend with benefits) is found in one of two ways. One, you go back to an ex-boyfriend or lover in some diminished capacity, where you hook up and try to enjoy the things that were good, and forget you're still ticked off about the rest. Or you meet some hot thing without a lot of prospects, and if you promise you won't fall for him and try to make him something he's not, you can enjoy sporadic, unencumbering carnal pleasure.

You're the island in the stream for each other, just like Dolly Parton and Kenny Rogers sang in that hokey 80's ballad…. "islands in the stream, that is what we are…we rely on each other from one lover to another…" If the image of these two turns you off, the 70s and 80s provided many other sexual theme songs….*if you want my body and you think I'm sexy, we've got tonight, let's get it on, you shook me all night long, tonights the night*. Notice these are all songs sung by men….

I know in the age of AIDs, we are supposed to have a return to sexual modesty. It's certainly prudent. Like most women, I was raised to think that men always want sex and that women control it. That any woman, so long as she was not physically revolting, could get laid anytime. She could go to a bar, chat up a cute guy, and so long as he wasn't gay, happily married or particularly moral, she could get lucky that night. Now that I am older, I see that is just not true. Because she's the one who can't bring herself to go there.

I know so many wonderful women who want a lover, but they aren't going to sleep with just anyone. What they really want is sexual expression in a committed relationship. And they aren't in one. So what are they to do? There are all kinds of hobbies, trips to take, friends to see. Yes, there are. But our time on this earth is limited. Do you really want to live without passion in your life?

I was watching *Sex and the City* reruns recently. I've seen every episode five times and I still enjoy them. This was one of the episodes when Samantha tells the women how fabulous they all are- they have great jobs, great apartments, great sex. They all seem to be getting action on that show, wherever and whenever they want. Except for Miranda- she's the only character who openly complains about the lack of prospects. She's the most honest.

I know this is TV, not real life, and that the success of the show was that it was a fantasy of great girlfriends AND great male prospects. New male characters kept coming in, all willing to take the role assigned to them by women. They all had a nickname, and served a certain purpose. But despite how fun the show was, it helped to set unreal expectations for real single women. In real life, male leads don't continually show up and they don't just exit stage left when you're done with them. In real life, the supply rarely meets the demand.

The reason for this supply barrier in large part rests with us. As the years go by, it is not so easy to even find someone you want to sleep with. I'm long past the point of finding a guy hot and just running with it. While I never had to have commitment to sleep with a man, but there had to be consistency. I didn't want to create a desire for something that won't be able to be sated because the guy stopped calling me.

Also, what I find attractive is more complex than it used to be. There was a time, way back, when it was almost all physical. The shape of his body, the cut of his hair, his dark eyes and surly grin. But now, if a guy opens his mouth and he's angry, or dim-witted, or shallow, that just ends it for me. I won't enjoy getting it on with him, so why do it? The cross hairs of lust center on far fewer targets these days.

There are all kinds of web sites now devoted to casual sexual encounters, where women can go on, post a picture and within a half hour be meeting someone for coffee and whatever else. Theoretically, that may be great, and we talk about sexual liberation and being able to choose, but sometimes getting healthy emotionally means you just wouldn't do something like that. You want to share your body with someone who knows and cares for you.

And… we all have a little more self respect now. When you like yourself, you want to spend your time where it is best spent. With someone who appreciates you, and who has something to offer himself. You don't give yourself away anymore. It's like a good diet. If you're going to consume the calories, you'd rather have the crème brule in a French restaurant than the 60 cents Snickers bar.

It's gotten harder to get down and dirty. I don't have a moral problem with one night stands. Sex is a biological imperative; it's a healthy and natural function of being human and adult. But there is still something tawdry about hooking up with a stranger. It's not so much the sex act itself, because that can feel pretty good. Not nearly as good as it is with someone you love, but still pretty good. It's more the whole scenario. Waking up, not having slept well because you had a stranger in your bed. Or you were in his bed and now you have to go downstairs and meet his roommate or his dog. Do you have breakfast together or not? What if he doesn't offer you coffee, or take the coffee you offered? Then there is the awkward way we try to convince him that we have never done this before. And the way you feel like crap when he doesn't call you again, even if you didn't want Round II.

I was talking to a client recently who felt she had found the perfect island in the stream- a 30 year old bartender she met out at a club. He'd called her, asked her to lunch. She was complaining "I don't want to meet him for lunch, I don't want to hear about his job or his dog. I just want to have sex with him!" I laughed. Any involvement requires a certain amount of effort. It just does. And you have to really ask yourself if it's effort well spent.

Adventures in Cougartown

When I started this book, I never thought I'd weigh in on the relationship of older women and younger men. I didn't think it was particularly interesting. Sure, I'd dated younger guys. One even seriously. But there were never large age differences between us- a few years. Not say 15 years. And I was never looking for younger men like some women do. I wanted someone my own age. Who'd been through the same trials, had the same aches and pains, who like me, had grown through dealing with life's disappointments.

Then I met Guy. He was in my younger sister's group of friends. He was (is) European, tall, handsome. In his late 20s, but looked far older, around 35. And he was smart, funny, kind, successful- everything I was looking for in a man.

The first night we spent together, before falling asleep I panicked- that line from Rod Stewart's *Maggie May* kept running through my head...*the morning sun when it's in your face really shows your age*. Did my skin look like a peach that was left in the fruit bowl too long?

But when we woke at 6 AM, I got up, put my robe on, and headed to the bathroom mirror. I looked pretty good actually. Kiss-bitten lips, sex tousled hair. When we spent the next four hours after waking in bed, alternately talking and communicating in other ways, I thought what the hell. He likes me. I like him. I felt empowered, not diminished. He had no issue with my age- why should I?

Over time, I started to think, hey, I offer those qualities only older women can. I'm secure in who I am. I have interests and passions and I am looking for someone to have fun with. I don't need a man to complete me, or give my life direction. I figured women his own age would have nothing on me. My level of conversation, my cultural sophistication, my early middle age sex drive. I'm not emotionally demanding. I'm not playing games, pouting one minute, sexy the next. I'm not desperate for marriage and kids.

And I look good for my age. I take care of myself. I'm fit. I have long hair and cover up the gray. I'd like to think *I* look around 35. So why not take the gift being offered here? I have done everything I can to improve myself and be a better partner, but the right one hasn't come my way yet. Yes, I want a commitment and he likely doesn't, yet even if we were with people our own age, that might not change. My previous relationship was with someone my own age-Ian-and we weren't remotely in the same place about wanting long term commitment.

There is something to the older woman, younger man thing too. I see it in the faces of young men I meet at work, in class, at bars and at parties. Many of them are attracted to older women. And we to them. Most younger men today grew up with working mothers, and they seem far more progressive about women's issues than men my age. Often, older women have more energy and want to do more things than men their own age. A younger man can provide that. So other than the marriage-n-children issue, what's the big deal?

Maybe. I didn't want it if I was wondering what he was doing on a Friday night out with his college buddies. I didn't want it if we were hanging around with hot younger women who look at me askance. I didn't want the slight pang of loss when he talked about all the things that are ahead of him, those stages in life that for me have already passed by.

I tried to forget Guy's mother was only five years older than me.

I came to see that overlooking these things depended on me. My self confidence. My willingness to keep that open heart and open mind. That was what I really struggled with. For ten years, I was married to someone 10 years older. I was the ingénue. I spent those years feeling at a chronological disadvantage because my husband had been married before and had more life experience. Now I was older than the guy I was with, but I was still the one with the chronological disadvantage, because I'm a woman. Older women have far less currency, like we're past our sell-by date. Cougars. On the prowl for young boy flesh.

In the end, the relationship didn't work out. We were not in the same place. For a brief while, I was hurt and I missed him. But I got over it rather quickly, in part because I'd felt a built-in barrier to it ever lasting. My subconscious mindset was "He's too young, it'd never work anyway." But I learned something, as we always do from our failed romances. I learned yet again to take it for the gift it was. It made me feel sexy, desirable. I loved that despite our age difference, we had a lot in common and we really liked being together. Because who am I to judge who can love me? Or to say I can only love someone who meets certain specifications?

Under different conditions, it could have worked.

False Princes

It is bad dating conditions that seem to make some women turn to married men – they're out there, they're often looking, there is less risk of them wanting more than you have to give, your time together is special, a romantic interlude without the demands of a house and kids. Illicit, so it still stays exciting. Plus, you're free to see other people.

I don't condemn women who choose to be with married men. Who am I to judge? I do not think married men are fair game though. Not just because I was married. Not just because of what it does to his wife. Not simply because of the bad karma. We're talking about you here. You are still accepting far less than you deserve; you are still condoning his cowardly behavior.

I understand how sexually deadening the marriage bed can be, but if I'm going to choose someone wildly inappropriate, I don't want it to be someone else's husband. I'd prefer that hot young thing from the gym.

Though married men seem like an unencumbering option to some, there is always the high risk you will get attached. All those bonding hormones again. You want to be with someone you know you can be there for you. And he would want to know you were going to be there for him if he left his wife.

Even when you are both single, there is the issue of a man falling in love with you when that is not what you want with him. It seems like most men do not feel badly when they decide you are b-list. They are happy to sleep with you and enjoy your company, knowing you are not the one they want a permanent relationship with. But god forbid you want that! Right after my divorce I had several short term relationships I didn't want to make permanent. Our world views were too different, they didn't have stability in their lives, I just wasn't falling in love. But I was attracted to them and wanted to enjoy the right now. And my attitude was that we would have sexual exclusivity-which is healthy as well as less anxiety-provoking, but we were free to date other people. If you meet someone else you want to sleep with, I'd say, fine. Just tell me. And end it with me first.

This didn't always go over very well. Once, in a long distance relationship, I found out that guy was involved with someone locally too and just didn't tell me. Another time the man I was seeing seemed to have forgotten the arrangement and once reminded, angrily demanded "Oh, ok, let me get this straight. After three months of sleeping together we can DATE other people?" Uh, yeah.

Because what is your alternative? Never be involved with anyone unless you think it is leading to marriage, or living together? Maybe. For some people. But to potentially spend years waiting for that relationship to come along?

If you decide to keep it casual, the man has got to be willing to keep it there, and so do you. You can get together every now and then and you keep it fun and friendly, maybe even caring and loving, but you don't want to make it something it's not. But how do you say this? Without coming out and saying "I do want a committed relationship, just not with you"? Without sounding like a 70s cliché? *If you love something, set it free, if it comes back to you…It ain't me babe… I'm as free as a bird now and this bird you cannot change….*

They were on to something there, in those silly little songs that mark the inherent struggles with commitment. The dilemma of wanting companionship but not wanting to be trapped. The desire not to own or to be owned, but simply to belong. To have a home in another person. Even if it's just a rental.

I got into another such relationship several years back, and this time, things were different for me. I found I was thinking about him a lot. I was bothered that a week or two went by and I wouldn't hear from him. I wanted to see him more frequently and after I told him that, he didn't step up the contact. But I didn't want to give up what I had to get what I want. Then after feeling sad and powerless, I started to think you know, my job is to take care of me. And this situation isn't working well. *For me.* And rather than sitting around longing for his call, I thought I DECIDE what happens in my life. I can walk when the terms no longer suit me. And so I did. That feeling of pride in my fortitude far outweighed the pain of losing him.

I have spent the years since cancer treatment looking over my shoulder. Once you hear the word "cancer" you never forget your first gut reaction- *oh no, am I gonna die?* Everyone knows intellectually that life is short, but few of us get it emotionally, and have enough time to change what's not working in our lives. A little bit of sex and companionship goes a long way.

This was how I felt for many years. Yet as I've gotten older I've gotten far less able to enjoy something simply for what it is. I meditate. I try to live in the present. But I am ready for a committed relationship and have started to feel like "doing time" with someone is just wasting time. Keeping the real thing from heading my way.

Yet, the dilemma remains- what do I do until it does? Focus on my projects. Go out with friends. Travel. All those things that I do even when I am with someone. I also keep reminding myself that many great people are single. It's not like everyone has a happily-ever-after except me, or that there is something deeply flawed in me and that's why it hasn't happened yet. Being single may not be what I want. Because I accept impermanence though, I know this won't be permanent either.

This has been a chapter of laments. What advice can I give you except to say live fully and take the lessons life gives to you? Accept impermanence, in yourself and others. Accept that what is ok one day, may not be the next. Persevere. Stay hopeful. Rather than think everyone hit the jackpot but you, accept that everything changes. Bad stuff gets better, good stuff can get worse. Things come, things go. That is the gift of living in the present. No love is secure, except self love.

Only you can know how long to stay, and when to go. Or as Kenny Rogers says- you gotta know when to hold 'em and know when to fold 'em.

Scrapper 101

I ain't going let nothing get in my way,
no matter what nobody has to say....

-Mary J. Blige

I have an impressive collection of fridge magnets. My son's friends love to read them when they come over because they contain tons of sexual innuendo and a sprinkling of swears. Some of them are pretty bitter. One in particular shows two women talking and one says to the other "Once I thought I was a slut, but now I realize I was just acting like a man." Now that's pretty snarky, but therein lies some truth. Allow me to globalize here- in most domains, men are self serving. They do what is right for them. Eat when they are hungry, sleep when they are tired, tune you out when they are done listening....you get my drift. This may be the very quality that aggravates women the most-but there is something to be learned here.

Men don't abdicate responsibility for meeting their own needs. Take a romantic relationship. Men don't sit around waiting to be chosen. They want a girlfriend, so they ask girls out, and keep doing so until it gels with one of them. While some of this is cultural-men are supposed to do the asking-it's also will and self-determination. They don't sit around whining "Why are there no good women out there?" They keep looking, and if they get shot down, they keep on asking.

When a man does have a girlfriend, and he senses the relationship isn't going to last, he often won't end it. He doesn't sit around, obsessing about the relationship and how to fix it. He enjoys it, for what it offers, right now. He doesn't worry about "where is this going?" He just doesn't fall in love, or plan for long term commitment. In fact, many men will engage in an exclusive relationship, and string a woman along with the elusive promise of marriage. He may do this right up until he finds the woman he is looking for. Then he dumps the right now and marries the right one.

I observe this behavior with no malice. Every woman has been scorched by some ex-lover, and it is very easy to bash men. All men are assholes. But hating men isn't fair, and it's not going to motivate them to change. It's only going to keep you locked in negativity. Sure there are a lot of awful men (see Chapter Three). But there are a lot of great ones too. I truly believe that. So, instead of hating them for their self-serving ways, take a page from their book. Be a scrapper.

A scrapper is someone who continually looks out for number one - herself. Someone smart, resilient, always on the lookout for opportunities. Not someone who uses others, or is only out for her own gain. But someone who truly gets that life is short, and does her best to bring good things into her life, and help the bad things pass on by.

I know a man, Tom, who has fortunately for me always been just a friend. He is tall, good looking, well traveled, and makes a great living as a journalist. In the ten years I have known him, he has had at least six girlfriends, all of whom were smart and serious and stunning, in varying amounts across the spectrum. Any one of them would have made him a great wife. He lived with almost every one of them, too, but never got so far as to fully commit. No one got a ring. Then one day, out of the blue, he takes up with his most recent girlfriend's best friend, and within six months, they were married, had bought a house, and were expecting their first child.

Why her?

Some people might say it was just timing. Maybe. But before timing kicked in Tom was biding his time. Enjoying all the benefits of a girlfriend. Just not taking it to the next level. He must have spent many conversations dodging the questions "Where are we going?" and "Do you see us getting married someday?" Maybe he told the girlfriends they were not the one, maybe he didn't. But you can bet that with each one to his *own* self he was true. And in the end, he got what he was looking for.

I am no advocate of using people. I hope that Tom was honest with these women. Misrepresenting your intentions is always bad form. But after ten years of marriage and 10 years of post-divorce dating, I am a big advocate of women getting what they need, putting their *own* needs first.

That's being a scrapper.

A key trait of scrappers is that they are resilient. They don't give up at the first sign of failure. They pick themselves up by their bootstraps when they are knocked down. I love TV shows like *I'm Alive* and *I Shouldn't Be Alive* on the Learning Channel and Animal Planet. It shows us in stark contrast the difference between giving up and digging in. The show features people who were on death's door-lost in the wilderness, stranded on a remote island, stuck in a mountain crevice with a broken leg - and they conquer all these obstacles to survive. I watch these shows and wonder if I would have the tenacity and will they do. I hope so. And I hope that even though I'm not facing imminent death, that I have the tenacity and will not just to live, but to live *well*.

You have to learn to be a scrapper. I don't think it comes naturally for most women. We don't like to ask for things. We don't want to be pushy. We focus too much on other people's needs. On pleasing. Instead, we should always focus on our own life, all the time. Be considerate and fair, of course. But continue to assess what you are doing with your time, who you are spending it with, and overall how you are caring for yourself. Don't accept crappy situations! Know that the more you believe you deserve good things, the more good things will come to you.

We must particularly persevere in getting the romantic relationship we want. The better person you become, the better partner you attract. I hate when you hear a single woman say something like "Oh, maybe I'm meant to be alone" like no one picked her for the sixth grade kickball team. If she doesn't want to be solo, she shouldn't have to be. Love is for everyone. Persevere! Believe in it, will it to be, do what you can to make it happen. Don't lose hope and don't stop trying. Anything worth having is worth working for.

They say you meet people when you least expect it, when you're not looking. Yet if you don't seek you won't find. They're not going to ring your doorbell. I do know of one woman who met her husband when he knocked on her door with some mis-delivered mail, but I doubt that happens much.

So therein lies a dilemma. When you are looking intensely, you are trying too hard. When you don't look at all, you're not trying enough. What you need to develop then is some equanimity, some trusting nonchalance. When you meet someone you want to start a relationship with, you have to practice detaching, at least in the beginning. A little fatalism can stop those chattering monkeys in your head. It will either work out, or it won't. Be patient, rather than trying to force some outcome all the time. If you're meant to be together you will. If you're not, no amount of energy is going to will it to be.

We all have little bumps in the road of our relationships. Maybe he didn't call when he said he would. Maybe I'm going into the weekend without plans. I start spending all this mental energy on conjecture. I feel it as a clutch of anxiety, those fears of abandonment rear their crazy head. My mind starts a taped loop of questions: Why hasn't he called? When am I going to see him? What if he never calls? I waste precious hours when I could be doing something more fun and productive. Chatting with a friend. Working on this book.

A scrapper knows that she has to manage herself by managing her emotions. She has to talk back to her fears and anxieties. She has to tame them.

Every time your thoughts start to stray, you get caught up with the guessing and wondering about what is going on with HIM, redirect your energies. Stop that taped loop running through your head. Recognize that it is just anxiety over not knowing what's going to happen. There is no knowing. And you are feeling insecure because of that. It's ok. When I get in this anxious place, I've learned to stop, take a breath, and put my mind on something else by doing something. I might make plans for the weekend. Go for a run. Do the dishes. Take a nap. I try to meditate and get my mind on the moment. Right now. One minute at a time.

You need to be vigilant, just like with a diet. Even when you lose pounds, you can't just go "phew, that's done" and go eat what you want. Yet we know that just because you blew it one day, say ate a crate of donuts, does not mean it's caput for the plan. Eat better the next hour, the next day, the next week, etc.

Dieting provides another great example here. When you're restricting yourself, it always feels like a negative experience. It's a lot of "no, you can't eat that." And you're hungry, so you're thinking of what's lacking. Losing weight isn't just about eating less though. It's about adopting a new mindset. Learning to be mindful of what you eat, and to eat better foods. You can also adopt a new mindset about the single times in your life. You can not see them as a time of lack. This time can be peaceful; it can give you the blessing of clarity. It's not just something to be endured. You learn a lot about yourself during these fallow periods. You are gaining the gift of self-reliance, learning to trust yourself to take care of whatever comes your way.

When you trust yourself to handle anything, you can better accept what you can't control. First, we need to recognize our desire for control, and as said previously, Buddhism would tell us that desire is the root of all suffering. We want to know what's going to happen. But really, you'll figure it out when you need to. Trust yourself to meet the situation. The Buddhists also say if you can control it, don't worry because you have that power. If you can't, don't worry because there is nothing you can do. So breathe. And focus on the present. The past is done, the future isn't here yet. All you have is right now. Focus on the step that is right in front of you. We all know this stuff, but we forget how hard it is to be mindful. You have to keep *re*-minding yourself.

Creating a good life is about mindfulness in another way as well. We are all going to have bad days. We all have times when the relationship we desire is not forthcoming and we are just so very tired of looking. It is defeating. And even scrappers get sick of "the show must go on!" So take a break from looking. Know that about yourself- you're tired. You feel sorry for yourself. You need a break. Sit back and lick your wounds for a while. And plan for when you are ready to become a bootstraps girl again.

I have always felt that the right man for me was someone who I could be totally myself with. We wouldn't play games- we'd call each other because we wanted to hear each other's voice, we'd show our enthusiasm for the relationship with no ambivalence. I want the man with whom there will be no artifice, or withholding or manipulation…would that this were true! It is just not human nature to live without these tensions. At least some of the time. These conditions surface in other relationships. Power plays exist everywhere-at work, at church, over the dinner table, at the gym. People have moods, they act out, they take each other for granted. We want different things, or we don't know what we want.

As I said in the beginning of this chapter, I've observed that most men go for what they want, whether it be a job, a business opportunity, a certain woman. You've heard the saying that men are hunters. They like the chase. And they can be relentless. No matter how many times a woman has said she's not interested, it's not going to happen, he'll keep working it. Thinking some day she'll give in.

Women don't like the hunt, the strategy, the tension, particularly in romantic relationships. We want to nestle into a relationship, and get all comfortable. Spread out our things and just sit on the nest. Yet we have to accept that the hunt is part of the game. We negotiate at work all the time. High time we apply it to our personal lives. Think before you act. Play some hardball. Don't call him back right away. Let him wonder where you are every now and then. One of my favorite sayings is "get your hand off the penis and get your eye on the prize." The prize of course, is a good life. What are your relationship goals? Cohabitation? Having a child? It is so easy when you are caught up in a relationship to just be about the day to day. What are we doing tonight? How does he feel about me? When am I seeing him next? While these are legitimate concerns, they distract from the overall planning of where YOU want it to go, and how strategically you can best get it there.

To accomplish this, you have to always pay attention to how he makes YOU feel. Not what he seems to be feeling *about* you, but how you are feeling *around* him. Often we get too caught up trying to be what we think a man wants. I've had this scene playing in my head a million times – me on stage with the current man in my life. Watching myself laugh, stare with come-hither eyes, serve a fabulous dinner while wearing a lace negligee. It's like we have a witness, watching our interaction with the man in our life. She notices how cleverly I do some of those things, based on the man and what I think he likes. So easily, we lose our self-focus and get over-focused on the girlfriend performance, the role of "great girlfriend." Carly Simon recorded this song forty years ago- *The Girl You Think You See*. There was a line in the song "whoever you want is exactly who I'm more than willing to be. I'll be a queen, a combat Marine, a gypsy Rose Lee, to please you."

Sounds pretty subjugating. Fancy word for "whoah, have a spine there!" Yet we all have done it. You start dating a guy, and next you're saying "oh you like fishing?" Ok, well, I'll go out and buy rods and hit the river with you at 5:00 AM on Saturday. You're into buck hunting? Well, I think that's barbaric but ok, I'm heading to WalMart to buy an orange vest and some camo." Some of this is fun, trying new things, new roles. But there's a little sickness there too. It smacks of *I'll throw away my interests to spend all this time and energy on yours*. And he probably doesn't want that anyway, and would rather fish or hunt with his guy friends and see you later on.

Many married women do this too- they are golf widows, so they take up golf. Or spend every weekend on the boat or at the racetrack. It's fine if you want to share his interests, but make sure there really is something there for you too. There is nothing wrong with going off and doing different things. Time apart makes reconnecting all the better.

An over-reliance on pleasing men can keep you from becoming your best self. Nearly everyone wants a companion to share their life with. We know that. But you have to invest your energies into being the best partner to yourself first.

Ten years ago, when I left my husband, got an apartment, and entered therapy, I started buying a bunch of self help books. One of my favorite things to do after work, or after coming home from a date, was to fill up my claw foot tub with scalding water and get in and read for an hour. One concept I came across continually was that in working through your issues from childhood and learning to accept how you were parented, you have to learn to parent yourself. Your natural parents may not have been able to love you well, love you into a healthy self esteem, either due to alcoholism, drug addiction, disability, divorce, perfectionism, demands of other children, you name it. So as an adult you must learn to parent yourself. Give yourself that unconditional love and nurturing that you needed, and still need. And that will set you on the right path.

I think the same goes for romantic relationships. You have to partner yourself, put time and energy into that relationship just as you would a relationship with a man. Talk to yourself. Sweetly. Kindly. Talking to yourself, silly though it may sound, can be a real comfort. Take yourself out to nice dinners. Buy yourself nice things. I regularly buy myself flowers. I take myself traveling, several small trips a year, a big trip abroad every two years. I love to travel. If it's moving, I'm on it. Would I love to have some great guy to shoot off to the Caribbean with? Absolutely. Never been there. Hope to go with that guy someday. But I don't sit around waiting for it to happen. My life is not on hold. I take myself where I want to go. We all need to stop waiting for a guy to do certain things with. Many married women travel with girlfriends and leave their husbands at home. You may meet him and he hates to travel. So whatever it is you want to do- buy a house, travel, raise a child even. Do it. It's your life.

Another facet of this-and I know this may be trite even before I say it – you can't expect someone to love you if you don't love yourself. As many psychologists tell us, we teach people how to treat us. By what we say and do, how we project ourselves. By our body language, by how we treat our bodies. When I dated Nick, I learned the hard way that people who don't treat themselves well usually don't treat others well. So men with drug and/or alcohol issues, financial catastrophes, or other addictions are not likely *able* to be good to you. Maybe. Maybe they've worked on themselves enough. But generally, people can't give what they don't have.

Like many women, it took me a long time to figure out why I was staying with men who had nothing to offer. Sub-par creatures. People would tell me I could do better, and my rational brain believed them, but I was still hitching my wagon to men whose lives were not in order. I was like so many women who ask "Why do I keep meeting assholes?" rather than "Why am I choosing them?" Somehow I felt I didn't deserve better. We do this in many areas of our lives. We don't negotiate for a higher salary at work or leave for a better opportunity. We tolerate unreasonable demands from our families, or we put up with bad friendships and girlfriends who don't have our best interests at heart. It seems somehow we don't feel we're worth that much. And we are afraid of the risks of only having ourselves to rely on.

Going solo is hard. We need to admit that. Loneliness can be so strong it's like a physical ache. I particularly hate all those articles in women's magazines that talk about the benefits of sex-lower stress, greater concentration, better heart health, more good will, whatever. Sure I don't doubt it. But I know so many great women who would love to have sex with someone but it's not going to be just anyone. They want that physical expression in the confines of a caring committed relationship. Even married women suffer from lack- those whose husbands have lost interest in sex, or have a physical reason why they can't have it.

So another part of meeting your own needs is giving yourself physical comforts. There are the obvious routes of self pleasure, i.e. touching yourself. But there are other ways too. Do a ton of yoga. It really gets you in touch with your body and takes some of that ache away. Start hugging your friends more. Get a pet. Hug that pet a lot. Sit on the couch at night watching tv, have a glass of wine, cover yourself with a blanket or heating pad, pull the cat or dog up with you. Get regular massages. Make sure that when the last person touched you it was not 1995. Human touch is a key component of a happy life. Remember those news stories about Romanian orphans? Kids who were left alone in cribs in their early years, who had never been touched? They had attachment disorder for the rest of their lives. A contact-free life is not a great way to live.

Part of meeting your own needs is also accepting that not all relationships will last. Impermanence, yet again. I've always admired Margaret Mead, the prominent social scientist, who did all those studies of indigenous people in Samoa. In an interview once, she was asked something like "Here you are this brilliant social scientist, first woman to do this research, blah, blah, blah, but you've been married three times. How bright can you be?" Her response was wonderful. "Oh," she said, "it makes perfect sense. Seven to ten years is a life stage, and it's logical that the right partner for one stage may not be the right one for another." How true! You hope so. But sometimes it's not. A successful relationship is one that runs its natural course. Truly.

So how do you know when a relationship has run its course? It's asking if this man is growing with you. Is he supporting you the best he can? Do you share goals and want the same things for your relationship? I talk to a lot of women who realize they have been treating the man in their lives far better than he was treating them. When they realize this, they also find they had a role in it. They were giving things to him that they weren't giving to themselves- time to hit the gym, weekends free of family obligations, time to pursue his hobbies, etc.

In deciding who is right for you at any stage in life, it's crucial to first ask yourself what you have to give. Be objective with yourself. You are a commodity like any other, just like being on the job market. Who would be interested in what you have to offer? Some of this is building yourself up – you are worthy of love, any man would be lucky to have you and here's why....but some of it is being truly honest about your liabilities. Know thy strengths and weaknesses. Maybe you have a pretty face but are very overweight. Maybe you are needy. Maybe you have a great career, a beautiful home, wonderful friends, but such a fear of intimacy that the second things get a bit tough with a man, you bolt. Those are the gifts and liabilities you bring. What man is a good compliment to *you* that way? Honor your truth. I have worked way too hard on myself over the years to sell myself up the river so to speak. I have been with men who did not appreciate who I am. They loved me in their way. But some didn't get my sense of humor. Or wouldn't accept my generosity. Or thought that I was "too much." I ultimately left each of these men, because I had to honor myself. I am fully aware of what I bring to the table, and I've got a strong sense of what makes me appealing, to the right man. I'm funny, smart, attractive. I've got a great kid. I'm financially stable. Sure I have liabilities. I've been called arrogant at times. I can be intense. I have high expectations of people, higher than I should. I can turn hot and cold at times if you've ticked me off. Yet, rather than berate myself, this leads me to true knowledge of what I have to offer and what's right for me. Someone confident enough to take my ego, someone patient and communicative when I shut down. A woman who knows and likes herself gets a wonderful feeling of "sure you'd want me" that men find appealing. Confidence derived from self knowledge is a magnetic thing. Above all, honor your strengths and your weaknesses. Get a man who will honor them too.

Because at the end of the day, you will not be happy with someone who doesn't deserve you. The hardest person to love is yourself, but once you truly do, you can't settle for less than you deserve. When you know you are worthy of more, settling is not an option. Having to leave is often the price for self development. It seems the more you work on yourself, the fewer friends and lovers you'll be compatible with. Change has a cost that way. But you just need one partner. Not a million. There isn't a limited time offer on partners either. You can meet one at any time. But you do only have one self. Let it become all it can be.

The gift of age is realizing that every partner comes with some limitations, including you. Only you can decide if they are ones you can live with or not. Can you accommodate it? Maybe you will. Maybe you won't. Maybe today you will but not tomorrow. You change. And you have the right to reevaluate and change your mind.

I see a lot of women for whom the marriage bed turned out to be a bad investment. Yes, people do not always give us what we paid for. If this is you, ask yourself "What am I going to about it now?" Our society views a long term marriage as a success. Why? Just because it's lasted? So many women stay and make themselves miserable. Worst case scenario, they make themselves sick. Plenty of studies show that cancer and other diseases can be brought on by chronic frustration, repression, depression. No less than your life is at stake here.

There is another more burning relationship question, that is far more complex and harder to answer than whether to stay with a man or not. It's whether or not to become a mother. I think of another fridge magnet I've seen, with a woman exclaiming "oh no, I forgot to have children!" We all know that part of life *is* a limited time offer.

Sisterhood of the Single Mothers

Several of my friends do not have children and knew at a fairly young age that they did not want them. A couple of others struggled for years to get pregnant. A few more friends really wanted kids but never met the right man and did not want to do it alone, so didn't do it at all.

I doubt very few women *want* to be single mothers. It's certainly not a glamorous job. It has low pay, long hours, thankless, repetitive tasks, combined with the continued scorn of friend and foe alike. Everybody has an opinion on what you could be doing better. Society blames all mothers for how kids turn out, how much and how little you give them, in a way that they do not do to fathers. And "fatherless" kids are put down even more. We keep hearing that they become delinquents, drug abusers, emotionally troubled. Most single mothers are so tired trying to put food on the table and keep a roof over our heads that we have little energy left to give our kids, let alone to fight that stigma.

Despite the difficulties, I have to say, to me this is the most liberating act a woman can make, to have a child alone. To make sure she has the resources to love and care for that child the best she can, on her own. I say flat out to all those people who say it's unfair to the child-NO. I don't agree with you. I admit I'm biased here – I am the child of a single mother, a woman who left an abusive husband. My life would have been far far worse if she had stayed with him just so I would have a father around. I wanted one, I don't deny that, and not having a father created a certain boy-craziness in me, no doubt. And a certain low self worth. Yet I know plenty of women who did have a father around and ended up with the same afflictions. A critical, rejecting or cruel father can be far worse than none at all.

I have always wanted to be a mother. I wouldn't not be one just because I didn't meet a man. End of discussion. I was fortunate to be married when I had my son, and unfortunate I suppose that we got divorced. I have been so thankful over the years that I have a child. That even if I don't have a partner, I have the one relationship that was always the most important to me. I joke sometimes that I always knew I'd find the perfect man, I just didn't know I'd have to raise him.

Overall my son and I have a nice life. We do fun things - take trips, watch movies, go for hikes. The mortgage, the groceries and the utility bills get paid, by me. I make all of the decisions and while that gets tiring, I'm not arguing with anyone over them. We aren't subject to anyone's temper or foul moods.

For me, going solo financially isn't as hard as the emotional quotient. The loneliness. Thinking that no one cares about you, or your kids. Knowing that almost all major decisions are made by you, that you are ultimately responsible for all of it. You look at intact families sometimes and think I wish I had someone to play with my son like that. I wish I had someone else to make the dinner, run the bath, go to the parent/teacher conference. I wish I was going to family functions with a husband, then going home together, with him driving, not always just me. I miss the ease of sharing a home and life with a companion.

Until you walk by a husband and wife fighting then you think I'm so happy I'm going home alone to my cat and my TV.

A friend from my doctoral program said for years if she was still single by 38 she was going to have a child alone. The years went by, and that's exactly what she did. There are so many ways to do it. I know one woman who was artificially inseminated three times from the same donor, so she is raising siblings. Several friends have adopted from countries like China and Guatemala. A former colleague adopted five brothers and sisters from the foster care system. Two former clients got pregnant by ex-boyfriends. One by accident, one by request.

It takes a certain type of commitment to be a single mother. Not just to your kids, but also to yourself. To be vigilant about not letting that mother role be the only one that defines you. You are a mother, but you are a woman too. And likely a woman who still wants to meet the right partner. You need your own life. It isn't fair to you, or to your kids for that matter, to have them be your only focus. Kids are not an excuse not to build your own life.

There are now a slew of books that offer the how-to on single motherhood. In my experience, the following tips are the most crucial:

1. Find a schedule that balances both time for yourself and time with your child. You cannot sit home every night. You have to put some energy towards your personal needs. Even a weekly manicure or a few hours out with friends gives you the feeling that you are honoring yourself. And set aside special times each week with your kids. Even if it is making dinner or doing yard work, something functional, kids just want to be with you, and your supportive presence is going to give them the resilience they need to live a good life. In this case, it is about being there. Time alone and together *both* have to be a priority.

2. Find or form a single mom support group. I cannot stress this enough. Even if you know no one and have to post

online or leave a sign at a local grocery store, it makes a huge difference in helping you feel less isolated. When I was newly divorced, I was in a group of women where we continually shared a sitter for a Friday night out, went on camping trips together, pitch hit babysitting when one had a date. We were all in the same boat. Now I have a group where we meet twice a month for dinners. I also joined Parents without Partners, which is a group that offers tons of activities for both kids and parents, together and separately. This helps not only with giving you fun things to do, but with reminding you that you are not alone.

3.   Do less. Don't cook dinner every night. Pick up take out. Eat a bowl of cereal and take a multivitamin. When I had my son, my mother told me so long as your dishes are done, and your laundry is done, the rest can go to hell. Well put. The perfection syndrome affects all women, but single moms have even less time for it. Focus on what *needs* to be done. Maybe you don't entertain much, or you only have friends over who aren't neat freaks. A meal is a great gift someone can give you, or you them. Or just meet at a park for a picnic. Always keep it simple so that you can keep enjoying it.

4.   If you want a relationship, try online dating. I confess I've never liked it, but it is perfect for a single parent. You can "meet" people in the comfort of your own home. They know from your profile that you have children, so there is no awkward moment of trying to slip it into the conversation. As most people initially meet for a drink or coffee, a short time, it's easy enough to schedule it on the way home from work, or during weekend errands. If you are unattached, online dating can give you the sense that you are putting energy out there; you are meeting the universe half way. Don't let your tough schedule and parenting duties keep you from seeking a partner to share your life, if that is what you want.

Also, don't let your desire to be in a relationship make you settle just so you aren't raising a child alone. Some women choose men just so they can raise a family together, forgetting that parenting puts additional stress on the relationship. How many times have you heard about a woman who stays with an abusive man because of the kids? Or a couple who says they are "making it work till the kids go to college", like the kids don't see and feel the tension in the house? There are couples who said their marriage was struggling and they thought having a kid would help, yet it often makes the rifts worse. After children, it's harder to nurture the relationship when there are all these new demands- diapering, feeding, getting up in the middle of the night. Many couples also find they have conflicts around parenting styles. A lot comes out in the wash when you have a child with someone. So don't settle just because you want a father for your kids.

Settling?

I have a great friend who always quotes the Sopranos to me when I am complaining about some facet of my life. She quotes the priest who when Carmella was complaining about Tony's cheating, says "live off the good parts Carmella." I'm no Carmella- I didn't marry a mob boss and make my bed so I have to lie in it. But the sentiment is the same. Find a way to enjoy what you do have.

How do you live off the good parts? When you know what you will and will not accept. My grandmother always said that relationships are all a matter of what you are willing to put up with. I used to think that was so cynical. But as I've gotten older, it seems more and more true. Because is it realistic to believe that you will have everything you want with a man? I don't think so.

In a successful relationship, you must know your non-negotiables. In that pro and con list that all women tally in their heads, you must ask "am I getting what I'm giving?" How much is it worth for me to keep getting this, whatever it is? Settling doesn't work, but it's a lonely road to keep demanding something that may not even be possible. And here is where self knowledge really comes in. You know what you need and what would merely be nice. Now you can determine what is most important, and what you'll give to get it.

Single women are always told to keep a list of everything we want in a partner. I've had so many of these lists I can't count. As we get older, we recognize that we will not get everything on that wish list. Even that everything on that list might not be good for us. We also know some categories matter more than others. Like "kind" is gonna count for a lot more than "loves movies." As one girlfriend pointed out to me in my last relationship, it takes four qualities like "tall, well read, likes rock collecting, and appreciates my sense of humor" to cancel out one "has unstable moods."

When you're married, you are brutally aware of compromise. That is the engine that runs the machine of any partnership. You can't always get what you want. Every day you are dealing with the things you like and the things you don't. Competing agendas, ambitions, expectations. While we expect to compromise, we have to be careful not to use it as a way to deny responsibility for our own lives. We *have* to move for his job. He *insists* we do this or that. Yet you've got a choice, sister, even if you don't want to make it.

One thing I have observed with men, another page to take out of their book, is that men are far more accepting of their partners than we are. You don't see them always trying to change something about us. There are critical, demanding men, sure, but many more men seem to eat what's put in front of them, accept their wife or girlfriend's way of dressing, driving, entertaining, decorating, raising the children, whatever. I know several happy couples who've told me that what keeps them together is that they completely accept each other. As they are, strengths and weaknesses. I know several men who are madly in love with their partners and say it's because she gives him appreciation and acceptance and isn't trying to change him. Don't we all deserve that?

It's also not fair to expect a man to meet all your emotional needs. That's your job. You need to build your own life, have friends and family to spend time with, to support you emotionally as well.

I have lived long enough to observe, not just have heard, that the grass is not always greener. That what we think are the joys in other women's lives- their handsome husband, their beautiful home, their smart and healthy children-may not be as they appear. Countless times in my life I have been out at a restaurant or movie and seen an attractive couple holding hands and thought ah, I wish that were me, I wish I had what they have. I look at them and think *I want something that feels like that looks*....

And it may or may not be that way. As many times it was me out with my ex-husband, or a boyfriend on the wane, being miserable. We may have been kissing and holding hands, but an hour before we were fighting. I may have been sitting there trying to ignore that sinking feeling that this just wasn't working out. When some woman was likely watching me, wanting what I seemed to have.

When we see other women who we think hit the marriage jackpot, often this thought revolves around money. She landed a man who makes a lot of money. None of my friends or clients expect to be "taken care of", the oft used phrase that makes us sound like little girls. That's not what the women I know are looking for. We are savvy, though, to the fact that men often earn more than women. Even though we may not want or need a "breadwinner", we want a financial partner. If we are smart with our own money-we invest, we own property, we have a plan- it's fair to expect the same.

We all know past a certain age, we are going to have to accept some baggage. I hate that word, hate all the associations of someone showing up at your door with overstuffed suitcases of emotional problems, just waiting to be sprung. There needs to be a better word to express that none of us is unencumbered. I don't want to be considered to have "baggage" just because I have a child. The right man for me will accept my son, and be thankful he has come into his life. He will show him kindness and affection. And I would show the same to his children, elderly parents, even crazy ex-wife.

The older you get, the more you hear that the right man for you may not come in the package or situation you want. You'll have to take a chance on something less than ideal. He may be kind and attentive but he may have money problems. He may have tons of money, adore you, but he has four young kids from two marriages. It happens. You take some salt with the sugar so to speak. But what is a reasonable gamble?

It's all a gamble. We never know how "well" we can do in finding a mate, or if what we seek is even out there. I've had so many people say to me that I was dating down at one time or another. That the man I was with should have a better job, education, sense of humor. It is always easy to say to someone "you can do better." But is the better out there? I have met many friends' and clients' partners over the years, and didn't think they were right for them. Several eventually got married and so far, so good. Who am I to say?

Only you know if you are settling. Your girlfriends don't know, your mother can't tell you. The answer is within, and the answer changes. You're entitled to change your mind. Trust yourself to know when to move on.

No matter where you are in the process - dating, divorcing, despairing- recognize that one thing keeps us all mentally trapped-fear. Fear of being alone. Fear of not being able to take care of yourself. Fear of shortchanging your kids. Fear of never meeting anyone else.

We have to let go of all our fears and make decisions from a place of self-trust. You know you can handle anything life throws at you, good, bad or indifferent. You have strength and resilience won through managing life's ups and downs. You can trust yourself.

You're a scrapper.

Owning What is Ours:
The Seven Deadly Sins

Persons of strong character are usually the happiest. They do not blame others for trouble that can be traced to their own actions and lack of understanding. They know that one has the power to add to their happiness or detract from it, unless they themselves allow the adverse thoughts or wicked actions of others to affect them.

Paramahansa Yogananda

HOW TO BE HAPPY ALL THE TIME

Depending on which source you read, there are far more than seven sins, and some that are so obtuse you don't know what they are talking about. In the bible, they also cite "uncleanness" and "lasciviousness" as sins, as well as "variance" and "emulations" to name a few more. How can we stop committing them when we don't even understand what they are?

In this chapter, I am talking about the romantic application of the basic biblical sins: Wrath, Gluttony, Lust, Greed, Sloth, Envy and Pride. Because while men can cause us endless frustration, we can bring it on too. It takes two to tango. To create better relationships, we have to do everything we can to be good partners. So let's own what is ours. Let's not be that woman we know who's unlucky in love and we can see why.

Wrath (aka Anger)

If women's rage were a fuel, we would not have the current energy crisis. Most women I know are angry about something- traffic, co-workers, kids, menopausal weight gain. We don't often express our anger. We might eat it by stuffing ourselves with food or shop it away at Macys. We may be just a little too short with the people around us, or maybe we just complain a lot. Anger goes underground very easily. Because what woman wants to be seen as a harping shrew? Who wants to have people avoid them? Anger in women is considered profoundly unattractive.

I can't tell you how many times I have tried to stem the tide of anger coursing through my veins, simply because it was making me look bad, as well as making me sick to my stomach. I recall sitting in a therapy appointment one day and when I was done with my opening monologue, the therapist said "Wow. You sound like you're angry." Yes. Yes, in fact I am. It felt so good to be validated.

I think that's why 76% of divorces in the US are generated by women - because we get PISSED. Then we start thinking this relationship isn't worth it; he's an asshole; we'd be better off alone. Unencumbered. Over time, anger and disappointment turns to resentment and disgust, and one day we are just gone.

Some of our anger comes from what we can't control. Namely the man in our life. He did not take out the trash. He was flirting with another woman at a party. He spent your savings on a new jet ski when you already have one rotting in the garage. All legitimate reasons to be mad. But it isn't the legitimacy of our anger that matters here. No one is going to debate you on the merits of it. You feel it. So be it. But what are you going to do about it? Because let me tell you, it is only killing you.

Men get angry too, of course, and arguably their anger can be more dangerous. I have worked with angry men, and have even dated a few. See my little rhyme-y song in Chapter Seven about "Nick, and the DVD Player He Hit."

That was a real event. It scared the hell out of me when he calmly unplugged the DVD player, took it into the kitchen, and beat the crap out of it with a baseball bat. A few times he turned that rage on me by screaming. So red-faced and neck-knotted I thought he would hit me. It was just like being hit. Whack. One friend dated a man who had been a victim of child sexual abuse and had never received any counseling or help to address it. I have never met a more angry individual in my life. He was fired from several jobs for it, which only made him angrier. His anger had turned into hatred - of the people who fired him, the many women who'd eventually broken up with him. He didn't trust people, and he ran into a lot of self-fulfilling prophecies.

It is hard not to carry our childhood losses into adulthood and be angry about the things that were denied us. Yet, you've been around angry people, people yelling, raising their voices. At work, on the road. It's awful. You want to move away from them as fast as possible. I'm not saying that we all have to be happy-happy-joy-joy all the time, like a Stepford Wife. But we need to recognize that people want to be around upbeat people. They want *their* needs met. And don't want to have to worry about always satisfying yours.

Think about it. If you were a man would you want to come home to what my mother used to call a "puss face"? Someone already pissed at you? Someone you can't please? Of course not. No one makes another person happy, but you can certainly help make them miserable.

I have always said to my son- never marry a woman you can't please. I don't want him to choose a life partner who isn't able to be content or who expects him to fix everything wrong in her life.

There is a hidden gift to anger though that I want to conclude with here. When I feel anger, I try to stop and ask why I'm feeling that way. It's usually far deeper than the thing that just ticked me off. When I look under the surface, I usually conclude that I'm feeling taken advantage of somewhere in my life, or that I haven't carved any time for myself in a few days. And so I try to readjust that relationship or make that time as soon as possible. Anger's onset can be a good guide to how to live in alignment with your emotional needs.

Anger is an energy, as the band Public Image Limited said. So use it. Harness it for change. Let it help you get into a good dialogue with yourself about what is missing in your life and what you want to bring in.

Sloth

I don't know many women who commit this one. We are pretty industrious by nature. Maybe this applies only to men, lying on the couch, watching sports when they should be mowing the lawn. Ok- there is one area. Letting yourself go. When I read the bestselling book *Mayflower Madam* years ago, I was struck by madam Sidney Biddle Barrow's comment on why men go to prostitutes. On how women who are married often give up on looking good and start wearing old, tattered, ugly underthings when they should be wearing attractive, matching bras and panties. Hmm. Yeah. We all love to wear the rattiest clothes because they are the most comfortable. This really is a good book- matching panties aside, her overall argument was that we are not trying to be attractive anymore, and thus often aren't. And that is why men lose interest. Harsh, I know. But true.

Let's be honest. Sure, he should love you the way you are. But he is visual. And really, so are you. If he let himself go, you wouldn't like it. A fit, well dressed person is more attractive, male or female. We are all judged by how we look at work, at church, in stores, in the world at large. Why would home be any different? I'm not saying always wear a full face of makeup or rush out and get plastic surgery. Do what is comfortable for you. And do it for yourself. You should be keeping yourself up for *you*, not just your partner. You should look good so you feel good. So do what you're able to. Exercise and stay fit. Keep your roots dyed. Make sure your nails are cared for. Clothes are pretty cheap these days- stop wearing out-of-style things you wore 15 years ago. Take pride in who you are. Taking care of yourself shows self-respect and makes you a stronger, more confident person who brings more to all of her relationships.

Envy

If this book is preaching anything, it's preaching that no woman has it made. We all have joys and sacrifices. Pain and pleasure. You know you can look at the woman on your PTO board or who sits next to you on the subway, and she may have a great figure, a beautiful home, a handsome and successful husband…and when they go home he beats the crap out of her. You know that. You never know what other people's lives are really like.

What you should also know is what the occasional fits of envy we have are all about. They are telling us that this is what we want. Because that's why you're envying her. She has what you want. So now you need to get it. Rather than sitting around thinking "Who the hell does she think she is?" say "Way to go, girl! I'm going to get me some of that."

Women's envy of other women is a cancer. It makes you avoid your more successful friends, or snub the new woman in the book club. In the workplace, I've seen envy between women turn into sabotage. There is often a battle between the woman managers for the few positions of power, and a battle between female managers and female clerical staff. When I've dealt with this myself, I've wanted to go up to some women and say "You want this position so badly? Why don't you go get the degree so you can be in middle management?" As if it's an enviable place to be!

Bottom line, don't fight over the scraps! Any group, when it is divided, is less powerful. Infighting makes you weak. As women, we shouldn't waste energy fighting each other, but the societal forces that constrict us- lower pay, sexist attitudes, violence against women, etc.

We need to stand together to become stronger. That's how we won the vote, just 90 years ago. 90 years! Could you imagine not being able to vote, to own property, to have your own bank account? Of course not. But this was our great grandmother's reality. So support other women, and help them succeed too. Rather than operate from a famine mentality, believe that there is enough for everyone, for every woman to have the life and love she desires and deserves.

Lust

Well, if it's for shoes or clothes, you know its going to be a problem in your relationship. Credit card nightmares. If it's for another man, or another woman's husband, ditto. What I'm going to talk about here is the lust for *more*. We want a bigger house, a firmer butt, a bigger diamond ring. We are told bigger is better. Look at the reality shows out there- *Real Housewives*, *Wife Swap*, *Mob Wives*, *Basketball Wives*, *Southern Belles*, *Married to Rock*. They are all about who's got the better stuff. Our culture not only glorifies acquisition of stuff, but vicious competition between women over who's doing better. But as our current economy reminds us, that isn't a smart or even feasible focus to have.

We all know stuff doesn't make you happier. It doesn't make you a better person. It doesn't fill emotional emptiness. What it does do is get you on a treadmill, that no matter what you acquire- an Ivy League education, an oceanfront vacation home, a facelift- you won't be satisfied. There is always going to be someone who has more. So don't even hook into that game. Your energy is far better spent developing your physical and emotional health, the most valuable acquisitions.

Pride

I was born in August; I'm a Leo. I'm not going to deconstruct this one too much. Leos are prideful creatures. Pride can be a wonderful thing, because pride is what gets you out the door when someone isn't treating you right. Pride is what drives your work ethic, or what helps you foster happy, healthy kids. Pride is what helps create self-respect. I may have accepted sub-par behavior from men in my life, but I have always maintained my dignity and that shows pride in who I am and what I have to offer.

That said, pride limits us when it keeps us from being honest and present with a man. I have heard many women say they don't want things from their partners- more affection, more help around the house- if they have to ask for it. He should just know! Well, no one is a mind reader. Tell him what you want. Tell him how much it would mean to you. And whatever it is, give it to him first. If you want more affection, give it. More support, give that. Give and you shall receive. If you don't get it back, then you can make a clear, conscious decision. To move on. Either by getting busy with other things, or accepting it and not expecting more, or maybe ultimately by leaving the relationship.

The same goes for when a man hurts us or when a relationship ends. When you are hurt and angry there is always the temptation to lash out. Defend your pride. Hurt him as much as he hurt you. After breakups, so many women want retribution for their wounded pride. Yes. I get it. We all delight in stories of women sending their ex subscriptions to gay men's magazines, or in this era, flaming him online. My revenge fantasies are telling the small penised men I've dated the truth- you ARE really small and it really DID matter to me.

But who do you hurt in the long run? Yourself. Because it's even more energy that you are focusing on him. Acting on our wounded pride just keeps us locked in a negative cycle, at a time when our mind needs to embrace the positive. Endings happen for a reason. Let them happen. I tell myself that the loss of me in his life is punishment enough. He doesn't get to spend time in my life and in my bed anymore. Poor him.

In the end, there is dignity in always taking the high road. He doesn't get the ego boost of thinking you still want him. And you never have to worry if it is going to come back and haunt you.

Because you never know who knows who. Do you want to be out on a date and run into him or his friends? What if you apply for a job you really want a year from now and you find out the hiring manager is his sister and there goes that?

We haven't even talked about karma yet. This Buddhist concept scares me the most. You reap what you sow. Every action has a reaction. More specifically, everything that you do will thus be done to you, good and bad. Wouldn't you want to look forward to all the good stuff and not worry about any payback?

Greed

Greed can be like lust and gluttony. Never being satisfied with what you do have. Not appreciating the gifts in your life. Always wanting to have more.

I see this concept play out a lot during divorces. Many clients have told me horror stories of years spent battling exes for child support, visitation, or just simple courtesy. Sometimes I didn't think the client was being fair either, that they wanted to punish their former partners so much they ended up only hurting themselves and their children more.

Personally, I have had to make a lot of tough choices since I left my husband 10 years ago. I chose not to sue for custody and child support. I felt that even though we weren't working as spouses at that point, we could co-parent equally and my husband shouldn't suffer from not seeing his son. I wanted out of the marriage, so I moved out. Five years later, he remarried and moved to another country. This meant not only losing his help, but getting full custody and child support. We worked these arrangements out on our own and had a lawyer draft it. I could have gotten far more child support if I went to court. I hate putting my son on a plane so he can visit his father. I could have fought having to do that. But I want what is best for my son and that means finding a balance with what is right for his Dad too.

Many women have told me I am fool, and that I am being taken advantage of. Maybe. But I'm not greedy in that I have to have everything my way. I want what is best for everyone in what is a difficult situation. In negotiations, you aim for what is mutually beneficial. You give something to get something. You try not to just settle, but also not to *have* to win each time either. When you have to win, there is always a loser.

Gluttony

This is wanting too much of a good thing, which maybe is expecting one man to meet all your needs. Maybe it's about the Law of Diminishing Returns. The more we get the more we want then the less we get. If you are getting something good from a man, do your best to stop and simply enjoy it. Whether it's great conversations, or a wonderful weekend away together, don't always be thinking about more, or the next time. It's human nature to want pleasure and to avoid pain. And natural that when you have a great time with your husband or boyfriend, you want more. Why can't we do this more? When are we going to do it again? But try to be in the moment. Don't be a glutton. Take and appreciate what is put before you *now*. Tomorrow is another day. Trust that tomorrow has some good things in store and you don't need to worry about that now. It'll happen all on its own.

Let me throw another spin on gluttony - don't be a glutton for punishment. I have a client whose husband is a total ass. Horrible. Every time she makes a plan, a meeting for work or dinner with a friend, he refuses to watch their kids. On the rare time he agrees, he cancels last minute. Her youngest son is a pre-teen and hormones aren't helping his disposition these days. He sees how his father treats his mother, and he treats her the same way. He's sullen, refuses to answer when spoken to, refuses to at least occasionally act like a positive, pleasant individual.

My client is a kind, caring woman who works hard as a nurse manager, volunteers at an animal shelter, tries to keep the house clean and put good meals on the table. The people who should most support her are the biggest drains on her energy. She doesn't need the stress of dealing with their refusal to cooperate.

During one session, I gave her some advice. I told her that they are not going to change. They get a payoff from being difficult. And their payoff is that she tries harder. They know they have power over her, because she gets upset over their callousness and constantly tries to work out a solution. There is no solution when they don't want one. Except for her to get off the bus. Change her pattern. This is her husband. She has a right to some cooperation and respect from him. That is her son. He should communicate civilly with his mother. They are obviously not giving her this consideration on their own, so she has to take her power back. Not be so accommodating. Tell them flat out how things are going to be, what her expectations and boundaries are. And not budge on them when her husband and son inevitably push back.

Don't be a glutton for punishment. You'll only get more.

I hope this chapter highlights some of our negative actions in relationships. It's too easy to blame men for their failings, and not take stock of our own. Only by being willing to identify and then address how we "sin" can we grow and know that we are becoming the best partner we can be.

Hit the Road Jack

You must always know how long to stay, and when to go...

- Dixie Chicks

There can be no relationship book that doesn't talk about the bitter end. Any ending, no matter how overdue, is going to be painful. Whether it is your decision, or his, it is not going to be fun, or quick. And as we know, the only way out is through.

In my breakups, I have always wished for a quick and painless way to make those bad feelings GO AWAY. This is the time, if any, that I can understand why people do drugs– just to get your mind off of your life! At least for a few minutes!

When I counsel people going through a breakup or divorce, I can see the pain in their eyes, the anxiety in their bodies. I have been where they are, so many times that I developed a personal "break-up kit" of sorts to help me to get through it. Like the times in my life when I was looking for a job, or trying to lose weight, I pursue a set of actions that work for me.

After a breakup, I am not one to lie on the couch for a month with dirty hair. I do some wound licking– I eat fatty, sugary things. Watch too much TV. But I am the action type. Type A. Give me a list of activities to focus on; doing something gives me a sense of movement and accomplishment. That's what I advise people. Do something. Keep doing something. Make a plan. Make another plan, one minute at a time.

It may sound silly, but a personal break up kit is a commitment to care for yourself. It reminds you that you have gone through this before, and you know how to do it, how to care for yourself. You know how to help yourself move on. Going through breakups also shows you remain committed to finding the *right* relationship, and aren't staying in the wrong one just so you're not alone.

Here is my list of break-up action steps, garnered through years of painful experience. These are like those quick-n-easy recipes in the cheaper women's magazines. You know, like 1 cup of mayonnaise plus a pound of cheese and a chicken breast equals a great dinner for 10?

Scotia's No-fail Bakeless Break-up Plan:

Burn some sage in your home, a Native American tradition. Walk from room to room while it is burning, cleansing his presence from your space. Note though that this can smell a lot like marijuana so be careful who you invite over right afterward.

Get a massage. Let someone touch you. Let the massage therapist be the last person who touched you. Not your awful ex.

Do yoga. A lot. Unlock painful emotions from your muscles, connect to your body and silent the chattering in your mind.

Take scalding hot baths with a stack of self help books. Get advice to ease your mind and bath salts to calm your anxious body.

Meditate. Quiet the mind. Away from all those "How could HE dump ME?" questions. Even one minute of mental space will help.

Over process with a nonjudgmental and willing friend. Preferably one who has been through the same type of relationship with the same type of loser (this unfortunately is never very hard to find. A nonjudgmental friend is).

Walk. Fast. Or better yet, run.

Write in your journal, several times a day. Every sad little thought, put it in there. You get the release of expressing the emotion without overburdening your friends.

Write him the letter you'll never send. It really does work. You can get all your pain and anger out there, with no censoring, no annoyed or dismissive look from him.

Come up with mantras (*I'm beautiful, smart and funny; Grant me peace, free me from pain, bring me what I need and deserve; My right partner is coming to me now*) etc. Say them frequently.

Write down inspiring quotes and keep reading them (*A bad man is a gift that teaches you, through torment, to love yourself; better lonely and alone, than lonely with someone else*) etc.

Find one stupid phrase or object that sums up the idiocy of your ex. It might be something he said when he was crying, like "I feel like a little baby girl, with a diaper full of sand" (seriously, direct quote) or a smirky picture of him, or one where he looks pathetic. I saved a piece of the DVD player Nick smashed. I use it to remind myself he did me a favor.

Log on to Match.com or another online dating service just to see that there are thousands of available men out there. They may have problems, but they are at least ones you don't know about yet.

Play your list of breakup songs over and over and over. My favorites are *I Know It's Over* by the Smiths, *Love Will Tear Us Apart* by Joy Division, *It's Not Right* by Whitney Houston, *Since You've Been Gone* by Kelly Clarkson and *Fly* by the Dixie Chicks. They make me wail and dance, and they work every time.

Write bad rhymy poetry about him. Read to yourself and laugh. Repeat. Here's mine from the Nick experience:

Nick, and the DVD Player He Hit by Scotia Stone

I don't live in a pit

I don't do stupid shit

I don't pitch a fit

When you upset me a bit

I don't act like the barroom wit

From the stool where I sit

I have no dog, so no people it's bit

No anger problem, so no DVD player I've hit

I will not be submitting this to the *New Yorker*, but it did make me feel better.

When I asked a few girlfriends for their action list, one said "You forgot the most important one: Get laid - as soon as possible - by another guy. Then dump HIM." Yeah, I've heard that. The best way to get over someone is to get under someone else. Ha ha. Well, the verdict is out on this one. It certainly can change your focus away from him, onto someone else. It can give you a spring in your step- hey, someone else wants you after all. But it can also make you incredibly depressed, because usually this person doesn't know you or your body well, and your ex did, and you had that connection and history and now you have to start over, feeling even lonelier than before....so use this approach with caution.

Every woman should develop her own breakup kit to keep on hand. So if the bitter end occurs, she knows she can pull it out and get to work. When the going gets tough, the tough get going. This is self care- being a scrapper, always prepared to meet your own needs.

To start building your action plan, ask yourself what part of endings has always been hardest for you. What part of a romantic relationship will you miss the most? I always miss the physical part. This may sound awfully utilitarian of me, but the rest of the stuff I can procure somewhere else. I have friends and family to be emotionally supportive, help me around the house, do stuff with. I continue to see them when I am dating someone, so I don't have to play catch up when the break up hits.

The loss of physical contact and affection, for me, is the most devastating. When I'm in a relationship, I'm used to someone to keep me warm on the couch, because my feet and hands are always cold. Used to kissing, which I love. And I love all the other stuff I don't have to spell out here. I don't want to live without these things. As mentioned in the Scrapper 101 chapter, I hate reading all those stupid magazine articles that tell you how great physical intimacy is for your skin, hair, teeth, nails, well being, financial success, parenting skills, etc. I know I know I know. But what about those of us without a partner, forced to go without? Are we slowly rotting into the ground?

The desire for physicality has made me put up with far more crap than I should have. I have stayed with boyfriends just because the physical piece was still working. I've been there when that was **all** that was still working. And this brings me to the next analysis item. How much is too much, how much is not enough? When to stay, when to go. If you are in an Island in the Stream situation, where you know there is no long term commitment potential, does it matter as much say that he is still mooning over an ex-girlfriend? Or that he has somewhat racist and sexist views of the world? Sure, it's not what you want to hear. But is it a deal breaker? Doesn't it in this context make it easier somehow for you, so that you feel no remorse when you leave him?

What I do know for sure about breaking up is that there comes a time when a relationship is not worth the aggravation. It has become a bad relationship. No matter how much you may be attracted to him, no matter how much you want a husband or a boyfriend or a lover, if he is treating you badly, you've got to let him go. Your pride and dignity is worth more. You know the saying – there are no victims, only volunteers? Harsh maybe, but too often we let people mistreat us. We stick around anyway. So we should stop.

Not only should we respect ourselves enough not to tolerate bad behavior, we also must not take the blame for it. When a man is being manipulative or passive aggressive, don't think you did or said anything wrong. It's his to own. Don't try to cajole him out of it, either. It doesn't work. Maybe he's just bugging you, or you fell out of love, or you just know you'll never commit to him long term. If you just plain feel more drained than energized by this man at the end of your time together, then stop spending time with him. Your peace of mind is worth more. Breaking up is not the end of the world. It's just the start of a new search.

Women love to be absolute. This relationship is going somewhere or its not. I want to KNOW. But really you never know what is in the hearts of others. Frankly, you don't even know your own mind sometimes. It's confusing. And you can occupy both places at the same time. In love, but unsure. Sometimes feeling madly in love and other times feeling like you are going to stab this guy with an ice pick. We long to lock on to a person. This is my husband, he is *mine*. Now I don't ever have to search again. No. It doesn't work that way. Everything is impermanent. I've said this before but it bears repeating. Every day is a new day. Every day you decide.

I was in the grocery store one afternoon recently, rushing through between appointments. I ran into a former co-worker, who I hadn't seen in a decade. She told me she'd gotten married. I told her I'd gotten divorced. I was making a joke about our reversed situations, laughing, but she wasn't. She grew quiet. "How did you know when it was the right time to leave?" she asked. Ah, the question.

We divorced women get asked that all the time. While much of society may feel sorry for us, there are a slew of women steeping in envy. We did it. The hardest part is over. They haven't done it yet. We former wives have our own little club of freedom, with no dinners to cook, no guilt over the credit card bill, no cajoling him to take a trip with us.

I'm not saying it's a fun club, or that divorce is for the faint hearted. It's not. It's going to break your heart, be the death of your hopes, whether you leave or he does. There is a joke I've always liked – "why is divorce so expensive?" "It's worth it." Cynical, I know. But it hits at the cost of that choice.

Many women know they don't have to stay in a bad marriage or relationship. We can support ourselves. We can raise children alone. We can learn to date again, or to date for the first time. We have more respect for our time as we get older. We are not so willing to spend it with a man or in a situation that isn't working for us. Yet, I still see so many women "making it work." I never want to say that. Yuck. It sounds like indentured servitude. Do you want your man to say that about you?- "We're making it work"? I want a man who's with me because he wants to be. Who is growing with me, or if we're growing in different directions, we still find room to grow back together. Who if something isn't working for him, will tell me.

You should never punish a man for being emotionally honest. We complain that men do not open up and share their feelings with us. That we never know what they are thinking. Well, when men do overcome their fears of being vulnerable, looking less manly, when they are honest about their feelings for another woman, or their erectile dysfunction, or their failings at work, you have to listen and be understanding. Men fear telling us the truth because we may get angry or god forbid, hysterical. Yet truth telling is essential to any relationship worth being in. It's not always easy to hear. But be willing to listen.

As he should be truthful with you, you should be truthful with yourself. Many married women stay because the deal works for them. They like their lifestyle. They don't want to be alone. And that's ok. So long as it is a conscious choice. And not just *oh I don't deserve more* or *A great relationship isn't possible anyway*.

I know happy couples. I know people who light up when their partner walks into the room. One day I started feeling that if you know it is possible to have that, to have great love, why would you settle for anything less? It's one thing if no one got it. It was just a fantasy concocted by advertisers. But people do find great love, every day. We all can. There isn't a limited supply in the world, some women get it and some don't. You deserve it and you can have it too.

The price you will pay, though, is that you must continually maintain that open heart and open mind so that you're ready to receive love when it appears.

That Magic Moment

I've got nothing to lose and nothing to prove. I'm dancing with myself...

-Billy Idol

I love the quote - "be the change you want to see in the world." Mahatma Gandhi said it. Meaning rather than waiting for someone else to solve world hunger or domestic violence, you give it a try. Or while you still get frustrated by people who are mean, or rude, you make sure that you are consistently kind and considerate yourself.

It's a great credo on personal responsibility. We do have a responsibility to the world we live in. How we meet this responsibility is by creating the change we want to see in ourselves. When we become kinder, happier, more at peace, we make the world a kinder, happier, more peaceful place.

Life is the journey to create yourself. At the end of the day, you must decide how to construct your life, and be determined to do what it takes to live it well. Likewise, you can't do all the work it takes to get there then abandon it when a man comes along. The right man for you will see you in all your glory. He will appreciate the things in you that you know are great. Your stability. Your sense of humor. Your passion. Share who you are so that the right man sees that. Give your opinions on things. Be direct. Tell him what you know, and make sure he supports you in becoming who you want to be.

To have this authentic relationship, this true intimacy, you have to know not only who you are, but what you want in a partner. I looked at my wish list recently- it listed "funny, honest, affectionate, common politics, common interests, easy going", etc. etc. I've always said I wanted someone like me – responsible yet flexible, fun loving but not crazy, smart but not an egghead, fiscally prudent but not cheap. I want someone with the balance I have tried hard to achieve. Know your list well so that when he comes along you can check in with yourself about whether getting involved with him - either as the ONE or an Island in the Stream - is what you want.

As we get older our list has more non-negotiables on it and it seems harder to find who you are looking for. When you're young you think it'll all even out in the wash. You'll grow together. He'll change. The downside of choosing a partner when you're young is that you don't have enough life experience to know what will be a deal breaker later on. You may see signs of his drinking too much, working too much, flirting too much, but you have no benchmark. You can't see how much this negative trait will impact you years from now. When you are older you have the benefit of that wisdom, and know enough to know that certain things are not that big a deal. And certain things are.

Getting older is about the loss of illusion. In a good way.

When you meet someone new, and embark on a relationship, you always wonder if he's the ONE. You ask yourself "How can I tell if this is meant to be, if this will work out?" Bottom line, you can't. You have to get up every day and give it your best shot. Every day is a new day, so be prepared. The only control you can take is over your own choices.

It's your life. And you can't abdicate responsibility for it. You can't just wait around and see what the man in your life wants. We all do it- let him drive the bus. To where and what he wants the relationship to be. When I married, I really didn't have career goals. In looking back, I've realized that though I didn't admit it, the most important thing to me at that time was being partnered. Ironically, I probably wasn't a good partner myself then because I hadn't learned yet how to have my *own* life.

While there are many things in life we can't control, often we don't want to take control of what we can. It's scary to be in control. We want a relationship to solve all our problems so we won't have to struggle with how to craft a good life. Sometimes we're just lazy, or paralyzed by fear and confusion, and we sit around waiting for things to happen.

Many, many people choose to stay in unhappy relationships. Whether they're married or single. They stay for social and financial reasons. Because of family pressure. Because of fear. Those of us who are divorced have some advantages here. We've been there. We know marriage is not central to our existence. The divorced have learned another lesson too. Life moves on. Things get better. You can survive, and later, thrive.

Part of my maturing has been accepting that I did have a choice to marry young and move to another part of the country. I chose that, and all it entailed. I've spent many years coming to terms with this, and accepting how one choice always precludes another.

So many times I've heard women say things like "well, he doesn't want to get married right now..." or "I'd love to go to Paris but he hates to travel." As my grandmother used to say "Who died and made him boss?" You get to decide if that's ok with you. What do you want? A better way to frame these situations is "I've decided I'm ok with the fact that he doesn't want to get married now." Or "While it's not my preference, I've decided to go to Paris alone this spring." Reframing, sure, but it puts you in the driver's seat of your life.

When you make a choice, you still have to live in the unknown, the in-between times. And you have to trust yourself to be able to handle whatever comes your way. That is why you must grow into the happiest, most loving person you can become. So you are prepared to meet the challenges life will present to you.

For many years, a large part of me felt that great love wasn't possible. Like many women, I didn't have models for it growing up. I've also seen the worst side of relationships in the work I do. Divorce, court battles, abuse, abandonment. It's like the evening news- no wonder we all think the world is going to hell in a hand basket. All we see are the tragedies and traumas. We don't hear enough about the people doing great things for the world.

It's taken me a long time too not to judge every moment in my life by whether I had a man around, to stop thinking that the times without partners were boring, lonely times. Partnership has always been my central life goal, the thing I wanted above all else. But being fixated on it to the detriment of other goals has caused me pain and wasted precious time.

Letting go of the past chapters in our lives is a constant challenge for all of us. What is familiar is what is safe, no matter how awful it is. I had to learn to let go of the pieces of my past that were limiting me. Because the woman who lived in fear or felt she didn't deserve any better- I'm not that person any more. I am not defined by those fears and hurts. Many of us keep ourselves imprisoned by an old view of ourselves, thinking "I'm not that kind of person" or "I don't do those types of things." Who says? Maybe before you didn't run fast, give great presentations, or know a lot about wine, but now you do.

There is this strange thing about life that when it seems like nothing will change, that everything will stay the same, that is when it finally does. And then as much as you longed for change, your patterns will be disrupted and you will miss the security of what you knew.

Humans are amazing creatures. We can adapt to anything, survive any horrible condition. Concentration camps, genocide, enslavement, war. Yet we are creatures of habit. We work at the same jobs for 30 years, we wear the same clothes we wore in high school, eat the same foods, go to the same vacation spots. We fear change. Look at people released from prison, you'd think it would be the happiest day of their life, now life can begin again. But often they become horribly depressed, even suicidal. Because the structure they lived in, no matter how awful, was what they knew. It was a known entity. Comfortable.

The point of life is self development, shedding the skin of your former self to create your best self. When you honor your self, you don't get in or stay in bad situations anymore. Because you don't have to. You value yourself too much. And because you enjoy your own company, you're not afraid to be alone. You can operate from a place of strength and self-satisfaction in choosing a partner.

So how do you know when you find the right one? I think love means putting the other's interests on a par with your own. That you take care with each other; consider each other in all parts of your lives. You're a strong supporter, and a gentle critic. Because I know and value myself now, it also has come to mean a person I can truly be myself with, and who sees me for who I am. Not just who they want me to be or only as the persona I present to the outside world.

So how do you know when you find the one?

You already know. *You're* the one.

CPSIA information can be obtained at www.ICGtesting.com
Printed in the USA
BVOW072308141211

278413BV00002B/17/P